OECD REVIEWS
OF FOREIGN
DIRECT INVESTMENT

ITALY

ORGANISATION FOR ECONOMIC CO-OPERATION AND DEVELOPMENT

ORGANISATION FOR ECONOMIC CO-OPERATION AND DEVELOPMENT

Pursuant to Article 1 of the Convention signed in Paris on 14th December 1960, and which came into force on 30th September 1961, the Organisation for Economic Co-operation and Development (OECD) shall promote policies designed:

— to achieve the highest sustainable economic growth and employment and a rising standard of living in Member countries, while maintaining financial stability, and thus to contribute to the development of the world economy;

— to contribute to sound economic expansion in Member as well as non-member countries in the process of economic development; and

— to contribute to the expansion of world trade on a multilateral, non-discriminatory basis in accordance with international obligations.

The original Member countries of the OECD are Austria, Belgium, Canada, Denmark, France, Germany, Greece, Iceland, Ireland, Italy, Luxembourg, the Netherlands, Norway, Portugal, Spain, Sweden, Switzerland, Turkey, the United Kingdom and the United States. The following countries became Members subsequently through accession at the dates indicated hereafter: Japan (28th April 1964), Finland (28th January 1969), Australia (7th June 1971), New Zealand (29th May 1973) and Mexico (18th May 1994). The Commission of the European Communities takes part in the work of the OECD (Article 13 of the OECD Convention).

Publié en français sous le titre :

EXAMENS DE L'OCDE
SUR L'INVESTISSEMENT DIRECT ÉTRANGER
ITALIE

Foreword

This report examines Italy's foreign direct investment policies. It is the result of an examination held in November 1993 by an OECD Working Party made up of representatives of the Committee on Capital Movements and Invisible Transactions (CMIT) and the Committee on International Investment and Multinational Enterprises (CIME). These committees, whose members are officials from ministries of finance, foreign affairs, commerce and industry and from central banks, promote liberal, non-discriminatory investment policies through the OECD Code of Liberalisation of Capital Movements and the National Treatment Instrument.

The report has been reviewed and adopted by both committees and was derestricted by the OECD Council on 3 June 1994. Factual updating has been made through the first quarter of 1994.

Table of contents

Introduction

The 1980s were marked by sustained growth in the Italian economy and by progressive removal of obstacles to the free movement of capital, in particular to bring the country's regulations into line with European Community directives. In this favourable context, Italy experienced a substantial inflow of foreign direct investment (FDI) throughout the 1980s, and particularly in the latter half. Since the slowdown in growth in 1989, FDI flows have moved in contrasting fashion. Over the whole period, FDI grew at a faster rate than GDP, contributing to a growing proportion of gross fixed capital formation and employment. It was instrumental in modernising Italy's economy through the injection of new technology and management techniques.

At the same time, Italian enterprises reinforced their foreign presence considerably so that the Italian economy, as from 1979 and excepting 1987 and 1988, switched from being a net importer of foreign direct investment to being a net exporter. In fact, the investment stock held by Italians abroad has since 1982 been greater than the stock of foreign investment in Italy.

The growth in both inflows and outflows of direct investment strengthened economic ties with OECD Member countries, and most particularly with Italy's EC partners, the United States and Switzerland. This rapprochement, at the expense of the developing countries, particularly in Latin America, substantially altered the structure of FDI flows. Service sectors, in particular banking and financial services, showed spectacular expansion, notably on account of the liberalisation measures introduced in the latter half of the 1980s, whereas the primary and manufacturing sectors showed a decline.

Despite the scale of the FDI inflows and outflows, however, as a proportion of GDP they were relatively smaller than in other OECD countries. Since Italy has had no general control mechanism for foreign investment for some years now, and since sectoral restrictions have been appreciably relaxed, the explanation must lie in structural factors. The size of the public sector, the fragmentation of the private sector dominated by small and medium enterprises, together with the poorly developed stock market, may have helped inhibit foreign investment. The relatively high level of corporate taxation, subject to frequent changes, may also have discouraged some proposed investment in Italy.

The examination of the role of FDI in the Italian economy, and of Italy's FDI policy, comes at an opportune moment. Italy has recently embarked on fundamental changes to the direction of its economic policy. The ambitious programme of privatisation and de-monopolisation in many sectors of industry and services, possibly a lengthy process, is likely to generate new investment opportunities, especially for foreign enterprises. Italy is also making efforts to limit the weight of public debt. Over the longer run, that should make it possible to reduce the pressure on interest rates and tax levels. Changes in the wage negotiation system in 1992, and the abandonment of wage indexing, are among measures designed to reduce labour market rigidities and should help curb inflation. These developments, together with the depreciation of the lira since September 1992, should enhance the competitiveness of Italy's economy.

In the framework of this process of liberalisation and government disengagement, Italy has also taken a number of measures to open its economy up further to foreign direct investment. Privatisation, particularly in financial services, is an especially important aspect. Some sectoral restrictions applying to banking and financial services, radio and television, and air and sea navigation have been removed or relaxed. As part of the de-monopolisation moves, the monopoly of oil and gas extraction and energy production has been terminated and a more flexible mechanism, based on government concessions, has been introduced. The concessions have initially been granted to the enterprises which previously operated the monopolies. When the new regulatory framework has been decided and the enterprises are privatised, however, foreign investment should become possible in this sector.

Most of the recent measures to liberalise FDI apply only to EC investors. Investments by enterprises from non-EC countries are still subject to a number of sectoral restrictions, notably in radio and television and air and maritime navigation, and a further reciprocity requirement has recently been introduced in radio and television. Established non-EC investors do not enjoy national treatment in air and maritime transport, where Italian majority control of capital and management is required.

The Italian authorities have striven to develop international trade and investment by harmonising Italian legislation with EC law and practice, but more extensive changes are desirable to facilitate FDI.

The Italian authorities should notably seek to eliminate the sectoral discrimination that remains against investors from non-EC countries. The report also proposes that the new regulatory framework for the privatisation of industrial and service concerns should give non-resident investors and established foreign-controlled enterprises wide opportunities to obtain holdings, in particular by including the national treatment principle in the regulatory framework and via clear and transparent sale procedures. Italy is also encouraged to pursue its demonopolisation. Lastly, the report invites the authorities to continue to give priority to enhancing the general business climate and to strive to reduce the remaining obstacles to market access. The special incentives needed to attract investment to the less developed regions of the country should continue to be applied in a transparent and non-discriminatory fashion.

Chapters 1 and 2 analyse FDI trends in Italy, its role in the Italian economy, and Italian policy towards FDI. Chapter 3 concludes the report with an evaluation of the outlook for liberalisation in Italy. Annex 1 explains the nature and role of the OECD instruments in promoting liberal FDI policies and details Italy's position under these instruments. Annexes 2 and 3 present statistics on foreign direct investment in the OECD area.

Chapter 1

The role of foreign direct investment in Italy

A. Data and statistical methods

Until 1 October 1988, when the Act reforming the foreign exchange regulations came into force, Italy's balance-of-payments statistics were established on the basis of exchange control records.

Since this reform, the Italian Foreign Exchange Office (Ufficio Italiano dei Cambi – UIC) records foreign transactions on the basis of the compulsory declarations by enterprises carrying out operations amounting to L 20 million (US$13 300)[1] or more. These data are published by the UIC on a provisional basis in the monthly "Bolletino Statistico". They are subsequently transmitted to the Bank of Italy in order to establish the balance-of-payments statistics.[2]

UIC collects information about the size of the stake and the transactor's objective. To qualify as FDI, an investment must satisfy at least one of the following three criteria:

- establish a lasting link; and/or
- allow an active role in the management of the enterprise; and/or
- constitute a holding of 20 per cent or more in a quoted enterprise or a capital holding in an unquoted enterprise.[3]

Foreign holdings of resident commercial banks were included in the FDI figures until 1991; since then they have been recorded as banking transactions with foreign countries.

The statistics on stocks are obtained by summing the net investment flows, with re-valuations where appropriate for changes in share prices and exchange rates.

B. Foreign direct investment in Italy

The data communicated by the Bank of Italy on net foreign investment in Italy show a substantial growth in FDI inflows, in particular since the second half of the 1980s. The annual average growth rate between 1982 and 1992 was some 22 per cent,[4] much higher than growth in gross fixed capital formation (9 per cent) or GDP (11 per cent), explaining why FDI stocks were seven times the 1982 level.[5]

As shown in Chart 1, inflows were neither constant nor linear. There was substantial disinvestment in 1986, essentially because of Libya's sale of its stake in the FIAT holding company. The adoption of macro-economic stabilisation measures subsequently improved the business climate and brought a substantial inflow of foreign funds in 1987 and 1988.

These developments took place in a phase of buoyant expansion character-ised between 1984 and 1989 by average annual real domestic growth of 3 per

Chart 1. **Foreign direct investment flows to and from Italy**
1973-1992

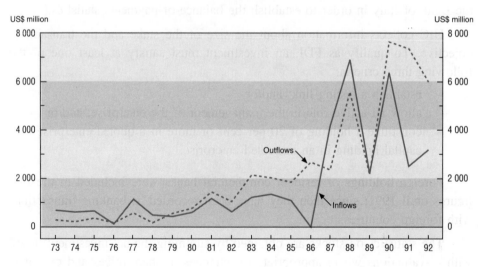

Source: OECD/DAF.

cent. At the same time, inflation fell from 12 per cent to 6.3 per cent. The two most dynamic components were private consumption and investment, particularly important in 1987 and 1988. These factors certainly had a favourable impact on FDI inflows.

Since 1989, FDI flows have moved somewhat erratically. This is partly due to the general slowdown in direct investment in the OECD countries since the late 1980s. There are also factors specific to Italy, however. The slackening of economic activity, the high level of domestic interest rates and the growing tax burden, the consequence of serious budget overshoots, and the appreciation of the lira in real terms, all weighed on investment decisions by national and foreign operators up to mid-1992. Since then, various factors, including the accelerated privatisation programme, the depreciation of the lira after September 1992 and more flexible labour market regulation, have promoted FDI inflows.

FDI as a proportion of Italian GDP had remained relatively stable over the period 1970-1980; it was lower than in the majority of OECD countries throughout the 1980s, particularly over the later years (see Chart 2). Only Germany and Japan had a lower ratio of foreign direct investment to GDP over this period.[6] The structure of Italian production, characterised by a large public sector and a fragmented private sector dominated by small and medium enterprises, could be one of the determining factors in this trend.

Significant changes are also to be seen in the geographical breakdown during the 1980s, as geographical concentration became more marked. The average FDI stock held by EC member countries rose during the periods 1982-1986 and 1987-1992, moving from some 49 per cent to over 52 per cent of the FDI stock. In addition, on account of the increase in FDI flows from other OECD countries (Annex 2, Table 6), in particular Switzerland, FDI stocks held by OECD Member countries totalled almost 96 per cent in 1992, as against 92 per cent in 1985 (Annex 2, Table 8). As shown in Chart 4, some 90 per cent of the FDI stock is controlled by seven OECD countries: Switzerland (22 per cent), the United States (14 per cent), France (13 per cent), the Netherlands (11 per cent), the United Kingdom (11 per cent), Belgium/Luxembourg (9 per cent) and Germany (9 per cent). Although FDI flows from Japan rose somewhat during the period 1987-1992, Japanese investment has remained low, around an average of 1.3 per cent for the same period. The absence of Japanese enterprises may be

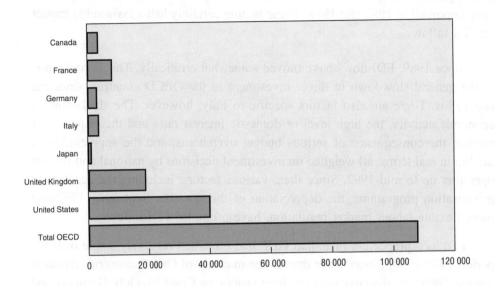

Chart 2. **Foreign direct investment in selected OECD countries, 1985-1992 average**
In US$ million

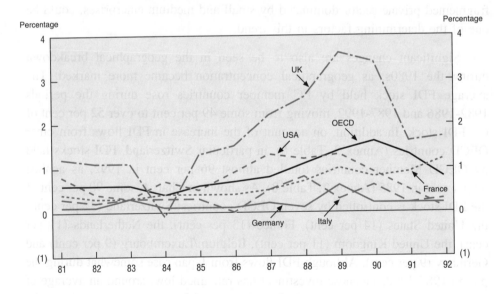

FDI inflows as a percentage of GDP
1981-1992

Source: OECD/DAF.

14

Chart 3. **Foreign direct investment into Italy**
Sectoral distribution

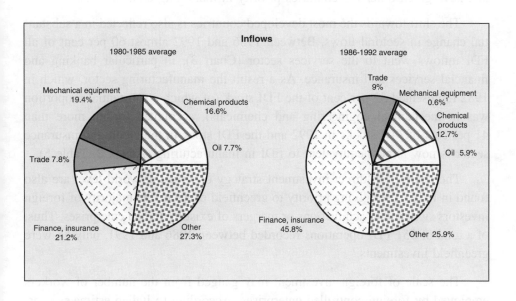

Inflows

1980-1985 average

Mechanical equipment 19.4%
Chemical products 16.6%
Oil 7.7%
Trade 7.8%
Finance, insurance 21.2%
Other 27.3%

1986-1992 average

Trade 9%
Mechanical equipment 0.6%[1]
Chemical products 12.7%
Oil 5.9%
Finance, insurance 45.8%
Other 25.9%

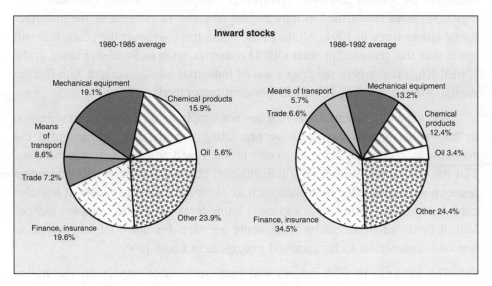

Inward stocks

1980-1985 average

Mechanical equipment 19.1%
Chemical products 15.9%
Means of transport 8.6%
Oil 5.6%
Trade 7.2%
Finance, insurance 19.6%
Other 23.9%

1986-1992 average

Means of transport 5.7%
Mechanical equipment 13.2%
Trade 6.6%
Chemical products 12.4%
Oil 3.4%
Finance, insurance 34.5%
Other 24.4%

1. Important disinvestments in 1986 explain the sudden reduction in proportion.
Source: OECD/DAF.

attributed to the fact that they are unfamiliar with Italy's language and culture and have given other EC countries priority in marketing their products.

The shift towards the most developed countries is also reflected in a substantial change in sectoral flows. Between 1986 and 1992 almost 60 per cent of all FDI inflows went to the services sector (Chart 3), in particular banking and financial services and insurance. As a result the manufacturing sector, which in 1982 represented 52 per cent of the FDI stock (of which a substantial proportion was in mechanical engineering and chemicals), accounted for no more than 41 per cent of FDI stocks in 1992 and the FDI stock in the credit and insurance sector is now almost equivalent to FDI in manufacturing (Annex 2, Table 5).

The changes in direct investment strategy observed at world level are also found in Italy. After giving priority to greenfield projects, the majority of foreign investors switched to acquisitions or mergers of existing Italian enterprises. Thus, of a total of 551 FDI operations recorded between 1986 and 1991, only 58 were greenfield investments.[7]

The scale of foreign investment may gauged from the number of workers employed by foreign-controlled enterprises. According to Italian estimates,[8] foreign companies established in Italy employed some 13 per cent of the manufacturing labour force in 1991. Although the figure has risen over the years, it is still lower than that recorded in other OECD countries, such as Sweden, France or the United Kingdom, where the proportion of industrial jobs associated with foreign capital amounted to 16, 18 and 23 per cent respectively.

It is generally accepted that FDI has not simply made a positive contribution to Italy's balance of payments by promoting exports, but has benefited the economy as a whole by bringing in new products and new production techniques. FDI has thus turned out to be a transmission channel for the results of foreign research in leading-edge industries such as electronics and chemicals. It has also contributed to the diffusion of technical know-how, notably in complex technological fields where licensing agreements are rare. Finally, FDI has helped to improve commercial techniques and management know-how.

The increase in FDI inflows and their favourable impact on the Italian economy, as observed following the liberalisation of exchange controls in the late 1980s, is likely to resume over the next few years. The proposed programme of privatisation and de-monopolisation in many industrial and service sectors

Chart 4. **Foreign direct investment into Italy**

Geographical distribution

Inflows

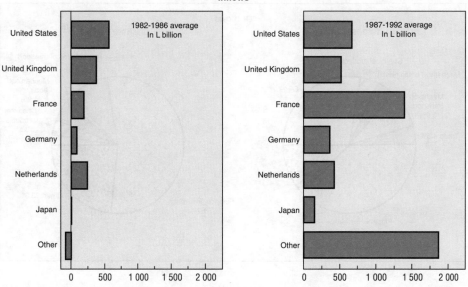

Inward stocks

1982-1986 average

1987-1992 average

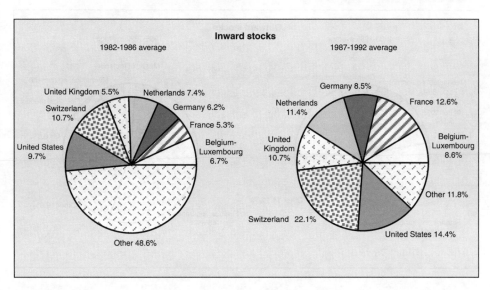

Source: OECD/DAF.

Chart 5. **Direct investment abroad**
Sectoral distribution

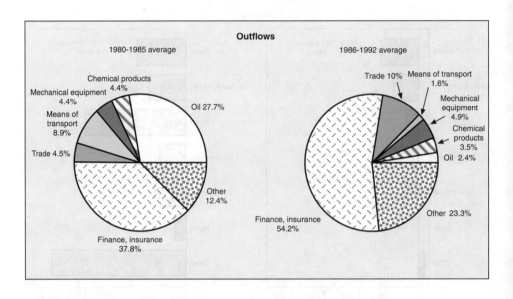

Outflows

1980-1985 average

Chemical products 4.4%
Mechanical equipment 4.4%
Means of transport 8.9%
Trade 4.5%
Oil 27.7%
Other 12.4%
Finance, insurance 37.8%

1986-1992 average

Trade 10%
Means of transport 1.6%
Mechanical equipment 4.9%
Chemical products 3.5%
Oil 2.4%
Other 23.3%
Finance, insurance 54.2%

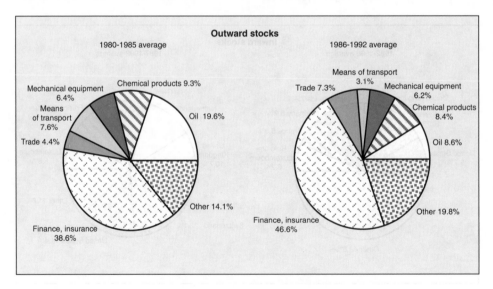

Outward stocks

1980-1985 average

Mechanical equipment 6.4%
Means of transport 7.6%
Trade 4.4%
Chemical products 9.3%
Oil 19.6%
Other 14.1%
Finance, insurance 38.6%

1986-1992 average

Means of transport 3.1%
Trade 7.3%
Mechanical equipment 6.2%
Chemical products 8.4%
Oil 8.6%
Other 19.8%
Finance, insurance 46.6%

Source: OECD/DAF.

may receive support from foreign capital. Italy is also endeavouring to reduce the weight of public debt and is keen to reduce structural obstacles to market access.

C. Italian direct investment abroad

Italian enterprises started to take part in the internationalisation of the economy at the end of the 1970s. FDI outflows, which grew at an annual average rate of 18 per cent between 1982 and 1992, were almost always higher than FDI inflows during this period (Annex 2, Table 1). The balance of the FDI stock has also been positive in most years since 1982 (Chart 7).

In 1992, some 80 per cent of Italian interests abroad were in OECD Member countries, as against 64 per cent in 1985 (Annex 2, Table 5). This geographical concentration, which results above all from the growing share of investment in EC partner countries (up from 38 per cent of the total FDI stock in 1985 to 60 per cent in 1992), was at the expense of Latin America (9 per cent of the total stock in 1991 as against 24 per cent in 1985). The main countries targeted between 1987 and 1992 (Chart 6) have been Luxembourg (17 per cent of the stock in 1992), Switzerland (12 per cent), the Netherlands (11 per cent), the United States (10 per cent) and France (9 per cent).

As Chart 5 shows, the sectoral breakdown has also evolved. Investment in the primary sector has been virtually dropped in favour of services (Annex 2, Table 2). Between 1982 and 1992, the primary sector share of total investment abroad fell from 22 per cent to less than 7 per cent, while manufacturing's share fell from some 46 per cent to 31 per cent. At the same time, direct investment in services increased to reach a level of 60 per cent of the stock of Italian investment abroad in 1992, as against 32 per cent in 1982 (Annex 2, Table 5). The credit and insurance sector particularly benefited from this shift, notably through investment in Luxembourg and Switzerland.

Despite the strong rise in Italy's direct investment abroad, its share of total OECD FDI is still low compared to the average for all OECD countries or for the larger EC states. The relatively low level of internationalisation of the Italian economy can be explained in part by the fact that public concerns and small and medium enterprises – which dominate its industrial structure – make little invest-

19

Chart 6. **Direct investment abroad**
Geographical distribution

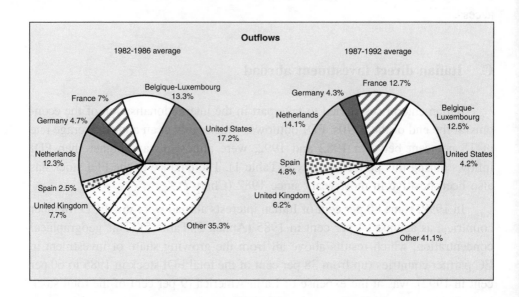

Outflows

1982-1986 average

France 7%
Germany 4.7%
Netherlands 12.3%
Spain 2.5%
United Kingdom 7.7%
Belgique-Luxembourg 13.3%
United States 17.2%
Other 35.3%

1987-1992 average

Germany 4.3%
France 12.7%
Netherlands 14.1%
Spain 4.8%
United Kingdom 6.2%
Belgique-Luxembourg 12.5%
United States 4.2%
Other 41.1%

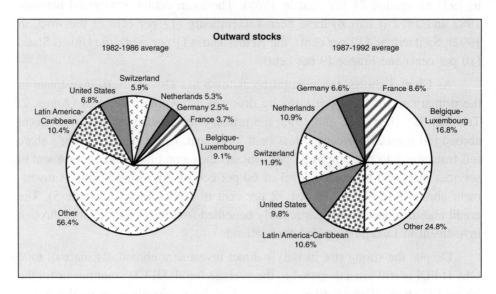

Outward stocks

1982-1986 average

United States 6.8%
Latin America-Caribbean 10.4%
Switzerland 5.9%
Netherlands 5.3%
Germany 2.5%
France 3.7%
Belgique-Luxembourg 9.1%
Other 56.4%

1987-1992 average

Germany 6.6%
France 8.6%
Netherlands 10.9%
Switzerland 11.9%
United States 9.8%
Belgique-Luxembourg 16.8%
Latin America-Caribbean 10.6%
Other 24.8%

Source: OECD/DAF.

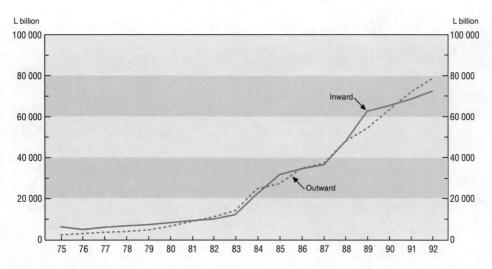

Source: OECD/DAF.

ment abroad. Foreign employment generated by Italian investors is estimated at 13 per cent of Italian industrial employment, virtually identical to the employment generated by foreign investors in Italy.

Chapter 2

Italian policy on foreign direct investment

A. Introduction

From a number of standpoints, Italian legislation on foreign direct investment is liberal. Foreign direct investment is subject to no general restriction and foreign investors face no authorisation or screening procedure. There is no restriction on the acquisition of land for industrial use and foreign holdings are limited only in air and maritime navigation, insurance, radio and television and the press. Profits may be freely repatriated. Grants for projects in economically underdeveloped regions are awarded on the same terms to both Italian and foreign-controlled enterprises. Italy makes no use of measures based on public order or essential security interests. Following the liberalisation of exchange controls in the latter half of the 1980s, Italy's financial system underwent structural reforms and substantial progress has been made to open up the Italian economy to international competition.

Further measures have been taken since then. Some sectoral restrictions applying to banking and financial services, radio and television, and air and sea navigation have been removed or relaxed. A privatisation programme has been launched covering a large number of industrial and service sectors. Privatisation of the financial sector is in fact an essential move not only to allow FDI in that sector but also to foster the development of Italy's financial markets in general, and hence the funding of FDI. The introduction of concessions in place of monopolies for oil and gas extraction in the Po valley and energy production was the first step in the de-monopolisation programme.

However, the FDI liberalisation measures have not always extended to investors from non-EC countries. These investors are still subject to a number of sectoral restrictions, relating to radio and television, and air and maritime navigation. Two further reciprocity measures have been introduced. In addition to the reciprocity clauses of the 1980s for the banking, insurance, hydrocarbons and tourism sectors, new requirements were introduced for radio and television as well as for minerals in 1990.

Investors may also face structural obstacles. Italy's industrial fabric is characterised by the predominance of small and medium enterprises and a restricted number of very large family or State enterprises. In addition, the Italian stockmarket is poorly developed. The combination of these factors substantially limits the scope for foreigners to acquire holdings. Institutional rigidities, such as limited competition and the extent of the parallel economy, may also operate against FDI.

The provisions of Decree 75/94, which apply in principle to Italian and foreign investors alike, grant special powers to the government as a minority shareholder.[9] Further legislation is likely to be brought in for the privatisation and de-monopolisation programmes. It may specify investment conditions in more detail.

B. Italy's industrial policy and FDI

Contrary to a number of other OECD countries, Italy has not pursued an active policy with respect to inward FDI. Governments since the second world war have generally opted for a "laisser faire" policy.

Accordingly, Italy does not practice any FDI screening policy and no special treatment has been provided. The first incentive programme, approved in March 1993 (Decree Law 78), is a modest one and does not alter the basic stance of Italian policy on FDI. It may be noted that, on account of budget restraint, the programme was not in operation at the end of the third quarter of 1993.

The Italian Government has taken a more interventionist attitude towards Italian investments in developing countries since the late 1980s. The main concern here is to improve the traditional aid system. Launched by Act 49/87, the policy rests *inter alia* on State holdings in joint ventures abroad via SIMEST (Act 100/90) and FINEST (Act 19/91), and on soft loans (Act 317/91). SIMEST, which has been operational since 5 June 1991, supports the creation of joint ventures in developing countries and in Central and Eastern Europe. It may take up to 15 per cent of the capital of joint ventures, and has to transfer its share to third parties within eight years of its first intervention. Soft loans are primarily granted for the creation of joint enterprises operating in sectors of strategic importance for the developing countries.

Industrial policy has accordingly been conducted mainly through the many enterprises controlled by the State. Present in all sectors of the economy, public enterprises are particularly widespread in the service sector. This is not in itself an anomaly, compared with other OECD countries, but Italy stands out by the number of services termed "public". At the same time, the State has an equally important role in industry (see Section C, below).

To cope with the difficulties of industrial adjustment, the Italian authorities have also made use of subsidised credit. It has been estimated[10] that aid to industry was on average, as a percentage of gross value added, 1.8 times as high as in France and 2.5 times as high as in Germany and the United Kingdom between 1986 and 1988. Capital grants, which have proved to be the main form of aid, have been concentrated in base metals and transport, in SMEs and in the Mezzogiorno or southern part of Italy.[11]

The economic imbalance between the north and south has been a fundamental concern of the government since the second world war. Assistance for the Mezzogiorno, granted since 1950, has gone without distinction to Italian enterprises and foreign-controlled enterprises wishing to invest there.[12] It has formed a not inconsiderable portion of overall financial aid, since it is estimated to have amounted to some 0.7 per cent of GDP[13] between 1951 and 1989, with a total outlay up to 1992 of L 250 000 billion. While this aid was not always part of a coherent overall strategy, it does seem to have encouraged a number of enterprises, notably foreign ones, to set up in the Mezzogiorno; by the end of 1991, for instance, 166 foreign enterprises with 260 establishments employed some 70 000 people there (14 per cent of the employment generated by all foreign enterprises).

Act 488 of 12 December 1992 and the decision of 22 April 1993 of the interministerial commission for economic planning (CIPE), both in line with EC regulations and directives, have superseded the Mezzogiorno Act. The new policy, to come into effect in 1994, will allow funding for investment projects for Italian and foreign enterprises in all zones affected by economic underdevelopment. As a result, regions outside the Mezzogiorno may receive financial aid, while some more developed parts of the Mezzogiorno itself, such as the Abruzzi or Latina province, may no longer be eligible.

C. Privatisation

The Italian public sector, among the most extensive in the OECD area, represented 19 per cent of value added, 24 per cent of gross fixed capital formation and 16 per cent of non-agricultural employment in 1987.[14]

Contrary to the trend in other EC countries, where the public sector was reduced by privatisation, the average share of the Italian economy taken by public enterprises remained virtually unchanged during the 1980s. The occasional sales of public assets which occurred in the 1980s were offset by new acquisitions, which were generally larger in terms of both turnover and workforce than the ones sold off.

Unlike in other EC countries, public enterprises are present in virtually all branches of economic activity in Italy. A classification of enterprises by net turnover shows that the State owns 12 of the very largest enterprises in Italy, and over a third of the top 50. As elsewhere, public enterprises are dominant in energy, mineral extraction, transport and communications, but there are also large numbers in industrial sectors such as plant design and installation, iron and steel, mechanical engineering, chemicals, synthetic fibres, electronics, glassmaking and foodstuffs. There is also very substantial State participation in service sectors including films, advertising, retailing, publishing, financial services and insurance.[15]

A number of legislative, regulatory and administrative measures relaunched the privatisation process in the 1990s. The 1990 Amato Act, dealing with the conversion of public banks into joint stock companies and the sale of up to 49 per cent of their equity to private investors, relaxed state control over public banks. Under Article 21 of Decree 356 of 20 November 1990, the government (Council of Ministers) could in fact authorise the sale of a majority stake in banks to private investors. Lastly, Decree 75 of 1994 terminated state control of all banks.

The recommendations of the ''Commission for the readjustment of public holdings and privatisation'', set up in 1990, were reflected in part in Act 35 of January 1992, establishing the statutory framework for privatisation.[16] Subsequently, together with the liquidation of EFIM in July 1992 (Decree 487), a great many public credit establishments, including Banca Nazionale del Lavoro, a specialised credit establishment IMI (Istituto Mobiliare Italiano), the IRI and ENI holding companies, and public agencies such as ENEL and INA, were converted into joint stock companies (Act 359). At the same time, ownership of their equity was transferred to the Treasury, which also has responsibility for the restructuring and sale of companies.

The actual privatisation programme began in November 1992, when the Treasury presented its "plan for the reorganisation of IRI, ENI, IMI, BNL, INA and ENEL".[17] The plan proposed the sale of the majority of the capital of public companies, public services and public financial institutions, and encouraged the management of these enterprises to sell assets by curtailing government assistance. Privatisation receipts were intended to increase the net capital of IRI and ENI, and to allow partial reimbursement of the enormous public debt by establishing a sinking fund.

Resolutions taken by the government and the Interministerial Committee for Economic Planning (CIPE) in December 1992 then determined which companies were to be privatised or restructured prior to sale. More transparent sales procedures were also agreed.

Banks, insurance companies and industrial enterprises showing a profit[18] were to be brought to market without delay, as these concerns did not call for any substantial restructuring. In addition, privatisation of financial services was seen as an essential step in the overall process, although the public offer for sale of major banks was to be staggered to avoid market saturation.

The enterprises which cannot be privatised for some time are the monopolies and state concessions and public enterprises in difficulty, where various forms of intervention will first be necessary.[19] For example, some companies need to be reorganised in order to separate public service functions and straightforward commercial activities. In other cases production and distribution need to be split and liberalised, and the degree of vertical integration must be reduced. Lastly, it is proposed to regroup and rationalise activities which are currently dispersed.

The main sales techniques envisaged in the CIPE resolution are sale by mutual agreement or private placement, plans for worker shareholdings or management by-outs, public offer for sale, and public auction. Apart from allowing greater transparency, public auction should impose greater discipline and make it possible to extend share ownership (to Italian households in particular). More complex or mixed techniques will also be proposed; for instance, a majority of the equity could be sold by private placement through competitive bids and the balance sold by public offer.

The CIPE resolution also provides for the establishment of "hard-core" shareholdings, to guarantee stable ownership. The introduction of special voting rights is also envisaged, especially in "strategic" sectors.

Given that Italy's stockmarkets are narrowly based, the involvement of foreign investors is seen as essential if the sales targets set out in the privatisation programme are to be achieved. Apart from Italian investors with hard-core shareholdings, where sales are restricted, all shareholders will be allowed to resell the shares they buy at privatisation. The consultants brought in to assess companies for privatisation have as a rule been foreign ones. The leading banks for the share placements have always included at least one foreign institution.

Decree 75 of 31 January 1994 defined the strategic sectors and set out the government's powers there. Article 2 stipulates that some enterprises in the defence, telecommunications, transport and energy sectors must amend their articles of association so as to allow the Treasury powers of veto for three years, over holdings of 10 per cent or more by any individual shareholder. The Treasury will also have powers to prohibit the dissolution, liquidation or transfer abroad of those enterprises.[20] In addition, Article 3 provides that those enterprises, and State-controlled banks and insurance companies, may introduce clauses to safeguard minority interests and clauses setting thresholds for individual or group holdings. These provisions apply in principle equally to Italian and foreign investors.

For future privatisations, investment conditions may be further specified. Ultimately the sole restrictions on ownership may relate to special aspects such as national security, or particular sectors agreed as exceptions under EC legislation.

The establishment of four independent bodies responsible for supervising the energy, telecommunications, transport and water distribution sectors, proposed in the privatisation progress report of April 1993, was still under discussion in the third quarter of the year. Under Article 11 of Decree 75, control of public equity in such concerns is vested in the Treasury.

In June 1993 the Ciampi government stepped up the privatisation programme by naming the concerns to be brought to market without delay. By early 1994 a portion of assets had already been sold off[21] and the procedure for selling a number of enterprises was well advanced. In particular, the sales of Credito Italiano in December 1993 and of Istituto Mobiliare Italiano in February 1994 were well received by the market. Public sale of Banca Commerciale was scheduled for late February 1994. Preparations for the privatisation of INA (insurance) were complete, and the public offer for sale is scheduled for June 1994. A number of steps have also been taken to pave the way for sale of ENEL (electricity) and ENI (gas and oil) in late 1994. The energy group Agip is to be sold early in 1995, and Stet (sub-holding of IRI specialised in telecommunications) later in the same year. [For further details of the privatisation plan, see also the OECD Annual Review of Italy.][22]

D. Control procedures

During the 1950s generalised controls were instituted in order to verify that foreign investment projects were of a "productive" nature. These arrangements, which ceased to be obligatory from the early 1960s, were officially abrogated in 1988.

Accordingly, unlike the arrangements in force in some other OECD countries, foreign investors in Italy are no longer subject to any authorisation or special notification obligations. They simply have to follow the same registration as Italian investors (notarised deeds, registration with the commercial court).

In the sectors where obstacles to access or reciprocity measures exist for non-Italian nationals (banking and financial services, insurance, air and sea transport, information – and more particularly radio and television and the press – commercial fisheries, the exploration and exploitation of hydrocarbons and minerals, tourism), all investors generally require a licence. Foreign investment in these sectors is controlled via this mechanism.

E.   Sectoral aspects

FDI in Italy is subject to a number of restrictions concerning banking and financial services, insurance, radio and television, air and sea transport and travel agencies. A preferential regime applies to investment by enterprises originating in EC member states.

i)   *Banking and financial services*

Until a recent period, the State controlled a substantial proportion of the banking sector; *de facto,* this limited access to the sector by foreign investors.

With statutory changes in the early 1980s, Italy's financial sector conducted not inconsiderable FDI. Banks were authorised to place some equity and bonds on financial markets. But holdings in the three banks of national interest by non-EC investors continued to be prohibited.

More recently, the financial services market underwent still further reforms. Without terminating State control of the public banks, the Amato Act of 1990 authorised the conversion of the public banks into joint stock companies,[23] and allowed 49 per cent of their capital to be sold to private investors. Since Decree 75 came into force, the Treasury is empowered to privatise the public banks entirely.

In addition, Decree 481/92, bringing into force the second EC directive on banking co-ordination (EC 89/646), abrogated the 1936 Banking Act which barred holdings in "banks of national interest". In line with the de-compartmentalisation of the banking system, the decree authorised universal banking and abolished the statutory and functional distinctions between commercial banks, which covered the banks of national interest, credit institutions under public law, ordinary credit institutions and savings banks, and specialised credit institutions.

The recent reforms, which should have a far-reaching impact on the structure and activity of the sector, also amended the rules applying to foreign investors. Holdings in Italian banks are no longer regulated, and are now subject to prudential rules only. The sole exception is that, for first establishment of bank branches by an institution originating in a non-EC country, there is a minimum capital requirement of L 12.5 billion.[24]

30

Incorporation of the second EC banking directive into Italian law has also relaxed the fundamental principle of Italian regulation concerning the separation between banks and commercial or industrial enterprises. Since Decree 481/92, banks can acquire holdings in non-financial enterprises, and reciprocally, non-financial enterprises can become co-owners of credit institutions.

However, such holdings remain subject to strict prudential rules:

- Bank holdings in industrial enterprises may not as a rule exceed 3 per cent of net banking assets and may not exceed 15 per cent of the capital of non-financial enterprises (banks with net assets in excess of L 2 000 billion may raise such holdings to 50 per cent of their net assets).[25]
- Holdings by a non-financial enterprise in a credit institution may not exceed 15 per cent, and may in no event result in the industrial or commercial enterprise controlling the credit institution. The approval of the Bank of Italy will be essential for all holdings of 5 per cent or more of a bank's capital.

These measures apply equally to Italian and foreign investors. But holdings in credit institutions by a non-financial investor originating in a non-EC member country are subject to reciprocity.

A new kind of multi-functional stock investment firm (SIM) was introduced in January 1992, following approval of the Stockmarket Act of January 1991. Under these provisions, designed to enhance transparency, efficiency and stability in stockmarkets, all companies dealing in securities have to have their head office in Italy. The Italian authorities have undertaken to amend the act in 1994 to bring it into line with EC provisions, some of which took effect after the SIM Act was passed.[26] It is unclear whether the new measures will apply solely to EC investment firms, or to all enterprises originating in the OECD area.

ii) Insurance

Insurance may be carried out only by enterprises taking the legal form of a joint stock company, a mutual company or, in the case of foreign-controlled companies, subsidiaries or branches. All enterprises, Italian or foreign, must obtain authorisation from the Industry and Trade Ministry to conduct life or nonlife insurance. In the past both branches could be conducted simultaneously by one company. At present enterprises have to opt for one or the other. Reinsurance is an exception inasmuch as it may be carried on by an enterprise not established in Italy.

The Italian insurance market, dominated by private companies, is characterised by a considerable State presence and substantial foreign penetration. The State controls four public enterprises. INA (Istituto Nazionale delle Assicurazioni), formerly a public agency, was converted in July 1992 into a public financial holding controlled by Treasury. The privatisation of INA, the third-largest insurance company in Italy ranking first in life insurance and second in general risk insurance, is scheduled for June 1994.

As the prospect of a single market in insurance neared, foreign investors forged numerous ties with local insurance companies in the latter half of the 1980s. In 1989 there were 247 registered insurance companies; 55 were foreign. In addition, one-third of insurance business in 1991 was written by foreign-controlled enterprises, mainly German and Swiss.[27] It seems likely that the foreign presence will increase following the privatisations.

In parallel with community directives on insurance, the Italian authorities have made the establishment of subsidiaries or branches of non-EC insurance companies subject to reciprocity.

iii) *Audiovisual and written press*

Under Act 416 of 4 August 1981, majority holdings in the press sector (newspapers, periodicals) are reserved to Italian nationals. This rule was introduced to ensure transparency in the sector, through the identification of investors. Foreign investors are restricted to minority holdings in this sector.

Under Act 223 of 6 August 1990, the State's monopoly of radio and television broadcasting was opened up to private-sector enterprises which are awarded licences. Under the new regulations, enterprises established in Italy or in an EC country may obtain concessions for the radio and television sector. Non-EC investors cannot have a majority holding in licensed companies, however, unless their country of origin offers reciprocal treatment. Lastly, non-EC nationals may not take holdings in licensed establishments with no legal personality.

iv) Air transport

The 1942 Navigation Code provides that authorisation to carry out scheduled air transport services may be granted only to persons or entities owning national aircraft which may be entered on the aviation register (Article 777). In order to meet the nationality conditions, aircraft must be the property of companies at least two-thirds of whose share capital is held by Italian citizens, and which are managed essentially by Italians.

The restriction on foreign holdings of more than one-third of the capital of air transport companies has, in line with the new EC regulation 2407/92, been relaxed for EC investors. Accordingly, EC country aircraft may be entered in the aviation register in the same way as national aircraft.

Regulation 2407/92 provides that air transport companies controlled by EC states or nationals can undertake cabotage provided that it represents an extension of an international service.

The establishment of ground handling facilities continues, on the other hand, to be the exclusive preserve of the State or public enterprises in Italy. At the same time a decision was recently adopted by the Competition Commission to open up certain services, in particular to foreign air transport enterprises.[28] A number of technical difficulties will have to be overcome, since some activities are difficult to separate.

Independent of the degree of control, the Navigation Code sets nationality requirements for the directors and managers of air transport companies. The chairman and two-thirds of the board directors must be Italians. While privatisation may bring changes to these provisions, no clear details are available at present.

v) Maritime transport

Like air transport, maritime transport is regulated by the Navigation Code. All vessels require permission to sail in Italian waters, and such permission is granted only to vessels on the national register; registration is in turn subject to the condition that vessels are majority-owned by Italian nationals or corporate bodies. On these grounds, requiring a genuine link between the owner of the vessel and the country of registration, non-resident holdings in Italian vessels are limited to 12 shares out of 24.

Except where international conventions provide otherwise, the Code also stipulates that cabotage is reserved to Italian vessels (Article 224). Since new EC regulations came into force on 1 January 1993, EC vessels are assimilated to Italian vessels and may be entered on Italian registers. Accordingly, they too may carry out cabotage. Services between islands are provisionally reserved for Italian vessels, however (EC 3577/92).

The Code of Navigation also lays down nationality requirements for the board of directors, over half of whom must be Italian nationals. The chairman and his deputies must also be Italian.

vi) Commercial fishing

In order to fish in Italian territorial waters, enterprises must be entered on harbour masters' registers (Act 963 of July 1965).

Given that the vessels used for fishing are subject to the Code of Navigation, only enterprises with an Italian majority holding may carry on maritime fishing.

In spite of recent EC directives on access to territorial waters for Community enterprises, this restriction also applies to enterprises originating in EC member states (Regulation 3760/92).

vii) Energy

The energy sector, in which public enterprises predominate, is heavily dependent on imports. In 1991 over 80 per cent of Italy's primary energy consumption was imported, including 95 per cent of oil and 65 per cent of natural gas. Between 12 and 15 per cent of electricity was imported, mainly from France.

The major public enterprises ENI and ENEL hold key positions in each sphere of energy activity:

- ENI, which has a *de facto* monopoly of natural gas production and imports, also has 40 per cent of the oil market. The remaining 60 per cent are shared among some 15 companies, some of which are foreign;

34

–   ENEL produces some 82 per cent of electricity generated in Italy, with municipalities and a few private generators covering the balance.

The rights of ENI and ENEL, which are largely sole rights, were set by decree. Legislation going back to the early 1950s set up ENI as the national hydrocarbons agency and gave it a monopoly for the construction and exploitation of hydrocarbons infrastructure and rights to prospect, exploit, transport and store hydrocarbons. Following the conversion of ENI into a joint stock company, it has been granted concessions and sole licences for most activities. Legislation in the early 1960s established ENEL as the public electricity agency.

The structure of electricity generation and distribution have not been fundamentally affected by amendment of the Act prohibiting electricity imports by importers other than ENEL, or by the liberalisation of electricity generation, especially for own consumption, under Community directives (Act of 9 January 1991), or by ENI's conversion into a joint stock company.

Prospection and exploitation of liquid hydrocarbons is subject to reciprocity for enterprises originating in a non-EC country (Act of 10 February 1953). Moreover, no operator apart from ENI may be licensed for more than 10 000 square kilometres on-shore or off-shore.

Since Act 221 of 30 July 1990 came into effect, mineral exploration and exploitation has been covered by a specific regulatory framework; a reciprocity requirement applies for investors from non-EC countries.

viii) Tourism

Authorisations, granted by regional authorities and endorsed by the central government, are required for investment in travel and tourist agencies. Authorisation may be refused to investors originating in non-EC countries under Article 58 of Decree 616 of 27 July 1977 and Article 9 of Act 217/83, which provide that foreign direct investment in "travel and tourist agencies" is subject to reciprocal treatment.

F.   Monopolies and concessions

Until a recent period, all major services regarded as public services were public monopolies.[29] Energy (electricity, hydrocarbons, nuclear power), telecommunications, transport (rail, air, sea, local), postal services, water, waste management and lotteries were all controlled by the State. This control was exercised either through public holding companies, which had *de facto* monopolies, or through exclusive concessions granted by the State or local authorities. The lack of separation between the regulatory authority and the public service producer to which exclusive concessions were generally granted made privatisation impossible.

Modifications have been introduced on account of privatisation and of alignment on Community provisions intended to expose the economies of member states to greater competition to promote efficiency and economic growth. These modifications entail the dismantling of State monopolies.

The first steps in this reduction concern the monopolies of oil and gas extraction and production. More flexible arrangements, based on administrative concessions, were introduced in 1992 (Act 359, Article 14). A new statutory framework for the sector is in preparation.

Despite the recent reforms, powers to assign, control and regulate concessions remain very fragmented and responsibilities are divided among a number of ministries, local authorities, public companies and national commissions, the most important of which is CIPE. In addition, there are no regulations defining the role that foreign investors may play in the de-monopolised sectors.

Public holding companies predominate at national level at present, due to the conversion of ENEL (electricity) and FS (railways) into joint stock companies.

Holding companies have the following government concessions:
- Electricity production and distribution has been entrusted to ENEL, and gas production and distribution to Snam and Agip, both sub-holdings of ENI.
- Stet and Iritel, two sub-holdings of IRI, control virtually the whole of the telephone network under exclusive concessions granted by the State.[30]

Only terminal and value-added services were recently liberalised in conformity with EC directives.

– A regime of virtually exclusive concessions also applies to rail transport services provided by FS. Certain local links of minor importance are exceptions to this rule, as are the construction and management of high-speed links, which have been entrusted to a new holding company (TAV) in which the private sector holds most of the capital. Domestic and international air services are provided by Alitalia, a sub-holding of IRI, under a regime of non-exclusive State concessions. IRI subsidiaries also predominate in short-sea shipping and motorway operations.

Public holding companies also operate in sectors wholly unconnected with the provision of public services, notably manufacturing activities, the distribution of salt and tobacco, mines and oil and gas extraction. Although there is no discriminatory regulation with respect to foreign investment here, all these sectors are *de facto* closed to foreign investment.

At local level, most public services are provided via public enterprises controlled by local authorities. This is the case with water distribution, waste management, and urban and inter-urban transport. The postal service remains an exception, being directly controlled by the State.

G. National security

Italy does not apply restrictions on foreign investment based on considerations of public order or essential security interests.

The predominance of the public sector has generally meant that measures to protect national security were not required. Given the uncertainties flowing from privatisation, this approach may be reviewed and government may have to seek new methods of retaining control of some "strategic" sectors, in particular by relying, as already mentioned, on exceptions set out in EC regulations.

H. Private practices and the regulatory environment

A range of practices or regulations can also have the effect, even if this is not necessarily their objective, of preventing or at least limiting foreign investment.

The main barrier to FDI in Italy is clearly the structure of production. Alongside the numerous companies controlled by the State, the private sector is highly atomised.[31] Apart from historical factors, relating to the tardy development of industry in Italy, the large number of SMEs is also due to institutional measures. Until 1990 SMEs enjoyed derogations from employment protection regulations and received fiscal aid. In addition, the inadequate development of financial markets did not assist the use of risk capital rather than self-financing or borrowing by medium-sized enterprises. Large private enterprises, relatively less common than in other developed countries, constitute less than 5 per cent of enterprises. In addition, joint stock companies often remain essentially family concerns with a limited stock market quotation. In order to prevent hostile bids, cross-holdings among owners of quoted family concerns are not unusual.

There has long been a general regulatory restriction on approval clauses in articles of association to provide a discriminatory reservation over sales of shares to foreign nationals, but under Article 3 of Act 75/94 enterprises in "strategic" sectors may now introduce approval clauses. Although non-discriminatory in formal terms they may, depending on the way they are used, restrict foreign investment.

It has also been estimated[32] that obstacles to competition such as subsidies and restrictive policies on government procurement have helped large public or private enterprises to build up dominant positions. Public enterprises are frequently in a monopoly position. Many public services are costly and of limited efficiency, financial services remain relatively little developed and retail trade, essentially in the hands of small enterprises, dominates the market because administrative restrictions limit the creation of new businesses.

It should be noted that antitrust legislation comprising a series of rules concerning cartels, abuse of dominant positions and mergers, was introduced in October 1990 (Act 287) in order to strengthen the operation of market mechanisms.[33]

In addition, the Italian tax system is globally complex and frequently amended. There are many tax rates, and tax is very progressive.[34] Corporation tax, a combination of income tax on legal entities (IRPEG, 36 per cent) and local income tax (IR, 16.2 per cent), amounts on average to 52.2 per cent. Taking account of the tax relief allowed for enterprises, the OECD has re-estimated this rate at 46.3 per cent, one of the highest rates in the OECD area.[35] What is more, enterprises have to pay heavy social insurance contributions and there is a considerable fragmentation of the tax on unearned income. The Italian authorities are aware that a reduction in tax, and in particular a more stable fiscal policy, would contribute to a better climate for business and have a beneficial impact on investment in general. On account of the scale of public debt, the government's margin for manœuvre is limited. But the Minister of Finance has mentioned the possibility of lowering the nominal rate while broadening the tax base.

The organisation of the labour market is a final element which, according to various surveys, is thought to have had a dissuasive impact on investment. Changes in the system of wage bargaining and abandonment of wage indexation ("scala mobile") since 31 July 1992 are moves towards greater labour market flexibility. But further measures still seem necessary to reduce the existing rigidities.

Chapter 3
Conclusion

Unlike some other OECD countries, Italy has no general control procedures and apart from some sectoral restrictions, the authorities have not conducted any active policy either to encourage or to restrict FDI.

Under the moves towards European integration and a policy of economic liberalisation and State disengagement, a number of measures have been taken to open the Italian economy up further to FDI. Restrictions applying to banking and financial services, radio and television, and air and maritime navigation have been removed or relaxed. It was noted with regret, however, that some of the liberalisation measures apply only to EC investors. Investment by enterprises from non-EC countries is still subject to a number of sectoral restrictions, particularly in radio and television as well as in air and maritime navigation. In the last two sectors, EC regulations (2407/92 and 3577/92) have a decisive bearing. Moreover, investors from non-EC countries face reciprocity requirements in banking, insurance, tourism and hydrocarbons. New requirements were introduced recently in radio and television and mineral exploration and exploitation.

The scale of the recent privatisation plan implies extensive participation by foreign investors. In the absence of a firm legislative framework, however, some uncertainties persist as to the real opportunities that will be available to foreign and non-resident investors. Examination of Decree 75 of January 1994 gives the impression that while the Italian government has relinquished the idea of taking an active role in industrial policy, it has not decided to forgo intervention in certain strategic sectors. The Italian authorities will have to introduce further legislation during the privatisation process. The new provisions should open the Italian economy up further so that direct investment can continue to contribute to its development, in particular by bringing in new methods and technology and different know-how, and through greater international integration.

The authorities have also undertaken to pursue their efforts to reduce the remaining structural barriers to market access which may have discouraged foreign enterprises from investing in Italy. In addition to the de-monopolisation and privatisation moves, efforts have been made to bring down the weight of public debt and over the longer term to reduce the pressure on interest rates and tax rates. The government has also shown readiness to develop financial markets and introduce greater flexibility in the labour market.

If the regulatory framework, already relatively open, is further liberalised, foreign enterprises may reinforce their presence in the Italian economy very considerably. Integration with EC partners, with whom closer ties have been established in recent years, may then accelerate and integration in the world economy will be strengthened.

Notes

1. Average rate of exchange for the second half-year: L 1503.9 = US$1.

2. OECD (1993), *Annual of International Direct Investment Statistics.*

3. At present this criterion can be used only for statistical recording of direct investment abroad.

4. Growth rate calculated from FDI inflows expressed in lira. Dollar inflows would give a different picture, depending on exchange rates.

5. L 72 570 billion in 1992 as against L 10 106 in 1982.

6. OECD (1992), *International Direct Investment, Policies and Trends in the 1980s.*

7. R. Cominotti, and S. Marchiotti, *Italia multinazionale 1992*, Etas libri, Rome, 1992.

8. Sergio Sgarbi:*Foreign Direct Investment in Italy: Policies and Trends*, Istituto di studi per la programmazione economica, Rome, March 1993.

9. Banca d'Italia, *Report on Italy's Privatisation Programme*, Rome, February 1994.

10. S. Laird, and A. Yeats: *Quantitative Methods for Trade Barriers Analysis,* Cambridge, Harvard University Press, 1990.

11. The Mezzogiorno comprises eight regions: Abruzzi, Molise, Campania, Puglia, Basilicata, Calabria, Sicilia (Sicily) and Sardegna (Sardinia).

12. Ernst and Young: *Regions of the New Europe: A Comparative Assessment of Key Factors in Choosing your Location*, 1992.

13. "Regional Disparities: the Southern Issue", in *Economic and Financial Situation of Italy*, Commission of the European Communities, Reports and Studies, No. 1, 1993.

14. CEEP (1990), Les entreprises publiques dans la Communauté économique européenne, *Annales CEEP*, Brussels.

15. OECD (1994), *Economic Survey: Italy*, 1993-1994.

16. This Commission established the statutory framework for converting holdings (IRI, ENI and EFIM), public agencies (such as CREDIOP, IMI and ENEL) and State monopolies including the railways (FS) into joint stock companies, and specified conditions applying to investment.

17. The plan was accompanied by a "greenbook paper on public holdings", describing the public enterprises sector in detail and analysing various aspects of privatisation. "Libro verde sulle partecipazioni dello Stato", Rome, November 1992.

18. The sixth-largest bank, Credito Italiano; the second-largest insurer, INA; the engineering concern Nuovo Pignone, which is part of ENI; and SME, the food sub-holding of IRI.

19. The government invited IRI to submit specific proposals for the restructuring of its sub-holdings Ilva and Iritecha; EFIM was to do the same for Alumix.

20. The enterprises concerned being designated by decree.

21. Part of the industrial activities of SME, a food/hotel/catering sub-holding of IRI, were sold off for L 747 billion; the glass specialist SIV, an EFIM sub-holding, was sold for L 210 billion; and some small ENI subsidiaries were sold for L 833 billion.

22. See reference 15 above.

23. A large number of the 142 public banks have already been converted into joint stock companies.

24. Establishment of a branch is assimilated to the establishment of a domestic credit institution, for which L 12.5 billion is required.

25. Fazio: *Implications for Italy's Banking System of the Transposition into Italian Law of the Second Banking Directive*, Bank for International Settlements Review No. 136, Basle, 27 July 1993.

26. The SIM Act runs counter to Articles 52 and 59 of the Treaty of Rome, the First EC Banking Directive, and the Investment Services Directive of June 1993.

27. Coopers & Lybrand, *The European Insurance Handbook*, 1991.

28. Financial Times, *Brussels Threat to Airport Ground-handling Monopolies*, 26 August 1993.

29. Europrospects Ltd., *Italy's Economic System*, 1990.

30. Les Échos, *Dernière ligne droite pour Telecom Italia*, 14 September 1993. Iritel was set up in 1992 with the takeover of an independent interurban phone company. Under a major restructuring plan, the telephone services provided by Iritel and two STET subsidiaries, SIP and Telespazio, are to be brought together under a new IRI sub-holding, Telecom Italia, since August 1994.

31. The Fortune ranking of the 500 biggest enterprises in 1989 included nine Italian enterprises as against 55 for the United Kingdom, 38 for Germany and 23 for France.

32. OECD (1991), *Economic Surveys: Italy, 1990-1991.*

33. Eric Lacey: ''The Italian Competition Law Compared with Other OECD Countries' Competition Laws'', *Journal of Public Finance and Public Choice*, 1990, $^2/_3$.

34. OECD (1989), *Economic Surveys: Italy, 1988-1989.*

35. OECD (1993), *Taxes in OECD Countries.*

Annex 1

Italy's current position under the Code of Liberalisation of Capital Movements and the National Treatment Instrument

Introduction

As a signatory to the OECD Code of Liberalisation of Capital Movements (the Code) and the National Treatment Instrument (NTI), Italy has undertaken a number of obligations in the foreign direct investment field. The present annex highlights the main provisions of these instruments as well as Italy's position under them.

The OECD commitments

The Code and the NTI are the two main instruments for co-operation among OECD member countries in the field of foreign direct investment.

The Code, which has the legal status of OECD Council Decisions and is binding on all Member countries, covers the main aspects of the right of establishment for non-resident enterprises and requires OECD members to progressively liberalise their investment regimes on a non-discriminatory basis and treat resident and non-resident investors alike.

The NTI is a "policy commitment" by Member countries to accord to established foreign-controlled enterprises treatment no less favourable than that accorded to domestic enterprises in like situations. While the NTI is a non-binding agreement among OECD Member countries, all measures constituting exceptions to this principle and any other measures which have a bearing on it must be reported to the OECD.

Member countries need not, however, liberalise all their restrictions upon adherence to the above instruments. Rather, the goal of full liberalisation is to be achieved progressively over time. Accordingly, members unable to fully liberalise are permitted to maintain "reservations" to the Code of Capital Movements and "exceptions" to the NTI for outstanding foreign investment restrictions. These limitations to the liberalisation obligations may be lodged at the time a member adheres to the Codes, whenever specific

45

obligations begin to apply to a member, or whenever new obligations are added to the instruments.

The investment obligations of the Code and the NTI are, in fact, complementary, both dealing with the laws, policies and practices of Member countries in the field of direct investment. However, the Code addresses the subject from the point of view of non-resident investors in an OECD host country, while the NTI is concerned with the rights of established foreign-controlled enterprises. Limitations on non-resident (as opposed to resident) investors affecting the enterprises' operations and other requirements set at the time of entry or establishment are covered by the Code. The investment operations of foreign-controlled enterprises after entry, including new investment, are covered by the National Treatment Instrument.

Measures pertaining to **subsidiaries** fall under the purview of the Code or the NTI, depending on whether they set conditions on entry/establishment or concern the activities of foreign-controlled enterprises already established. As to **branches**, the 1991 *Review of the OECD Declaration and Decisions on International Investment and Multinational Enterprises* introduced a distinction between ''direct'' branches of non-resident enterprises and ''indirect'' branches, that is branches of already established foreign-controlled enterprises. The latter are subject to all the five categories of measures covered by the NTI (investment by established enterprises, government procurement, official aids and subsidies, access to local financing and tax obligations). The investment activities of ''direct'' branches of non-resident enterprises, which concern the category of measures covered by the NTI, fall however, exclusively under the purview of the Code.

The Committee on Capital Movements and Invisible Transactions and the Committee on International Investment and Multinational Enterprises together conduct country examinations of Member country measures covered by these OECD commitments. These examinations involve a face to face discussion between representatives of the two Committees and experts from the country being examined. The discussion is based on submission by the Member concerned and a document prepared by the Secretariat. The objective is to clarify the nature and purpose of remaining restrictions and to identify possible areas for further liberalisation. The examinations usually conclude with modifications to the Member country's position and recommendations by the OECD Council to the Member's authorities concerning the future direction of the country's foreign direct investment policies.

Italy's position under the Code and the National Treatment Instrument

The FDI regime in Italy is a liberal one although restrictions remain in force in a number of sectors. Since the last country examination under the Code of Liberalisation of Capital Movements in 1988, Italy has pursued a policy of relaxing and in some cases removing a number of exceptions and reservations under the Code and the NTI.

Following the examination conducted by the CMIT and CIME in 1993, Italy has limited or withdrawn a number of exceptions and reservations under these two instruments and, as is permissible, added new reservations corresponding to restrictions introduced as part of the de-monopolisation of air transport, telecommunications and television.

As the attached list shows, Italy's exceptions and reservations are now confined essentially to investments by entities originating in non-EC countries in radio and television, insurance, air and maritime transportation, as well as tourism. The restrictions which apply equally to EC investors concern holdings in the press and publishing sector, purchase of aircraft, fishing in Italian territorial waters, and the establishment of stock investment companies.

In addition, investors from non-EC countries face reciprocity requirements in the banking, insurance, hydrocarbon and tourism sectors. The entry on tourism reflects a long-standing measure, inadvertently omitted in the past. New measures of reciprocity under the Annex E of the Code will be considered by the CMIT at a later date in the context of a general review of the problems raised by new reciprocity measures introduced by the OECD countries.

a) Italy's reservations on foreign direct investment under the Code of Liberalisation of Capital Movements

1. "*List A, Direct investment:

    I/A

    - In the country concerned by non-residents.

      Remark: The reservation applies only to:

      i) Majority participation or controlling interest in companies that publish daily newspapers and periodicals;

      ii) Licences granted to audio-visual communications enterprises having their headquarters in a non-EC member country;

      iii) Majority participation by non-EC residents in companies licensed for television and sound-radio broadcasting, and participation by non-EC residents in companies having no legal personality and licensed for television and sound-radio broadcasting;

      iv) The purchase by foreigners of aircraft registered in Italy and foreign ownership exceeding one-third of the share capital of companies possessing such aircraft;

      v) The purchase by foreigners other than EC residents of a majority interest in Italian flag vessels or of a controlling interest in ship owning companies having their headquarters in Italy;

vi) The purchase of Italian flag vessels used to fish in Italian territorial waters;

vii) The establishment of branches, agencies, etc. of securities investment companies.''

2. Italy's position under Annex E to the Code of Liberalisation of Capital Movements:

'' *i)* Establishment of branches of banks originating in non-EC member countries is subject to a reciprocity requirement;

ii) Establishment of insurance companies originating in non-EC member countries is subject to a reciprocity requirement;

iii) Foreign investment in the exploration and exploitation of liquid and gaseous hydrocarbons is subject to a reciprocity requirement;

iv) The granting of licences to tour operators or travel agents who are nationals of non-EC member countries, or to enterprises in such countries, is subject to a reciprocity requirement.''

b) *Measures reported as exceptions to the National Treatment Instrument*

A. Exceptions at national level

I. Investment by established foreign-controlled enterprises

Fishing

Fishing in territorial waters reserved to nationals.

Authority: Act No. 963 of July 1965; Article 2 of the Convention on territorial waters and the contiguous zone of April 1958.

Air transport

Cabotage is reserved to national companies unless international conventions on air transport services state otherwise.

Companies from EC countries are authorised to undertake cabotage that represents an extension of an international service.

Authority: Navigation Code, Article 780 of RD No. 327 of March 1942.

Air transport

Registration of aircraft is reserved for Italian citizens, the State, Provinces, State authorities and institutions, and companies headquartered in Italy, with at least two-thirds of the share capital owned by Italian citizens.

Air transport companies holding licences issued in Italy are subject to the nationality requirements established by Regulation 2407/92, which provides for the control of enterprises by EC States or Community citizens.

Authority: Navigation Code, Article 751 of RD No. 327 of March 1942.

Air transport

Non-national airlines are not permitted to establish their own ground handling facilities in airports which are either directly managed by the State or awarded in partial concession to companies with essentially public capital.

Authority: Decree of the Ministry of Transport No. 28/T of March 1988 in application of Article 7 of Act No. 449 of August 1985.

Maritime transport

Maritime cabotage as well as maritime services of port areas are reserved for Italian- and Community-owned ships. Cabotage between islands remains exclusively reserved for Italian ships.

Authority: Article 224 of the Code of Navigation.

II.   Official aids and subsidies

Films

Aids, subsidies and credit facilities are available for Italian film production or co-production with foreign-controlled enterprises from countries with co-production agreements. Credit facilities may also be awarded for the distribution of films by Italian-owned companies. EC companies are assimilated to Italian companies.

III.   Tax obligations

None.

IV.   Government purchasing

None.

V. Access to local finance

None.

B. Exceptions by territorial subdivisions

None.

c) Measures reported for transparency under the National Treatment Instrument

A. Transparency measures at the level of national government

I. Measures based on public order and essential security considerations.

None.

II. Other measures reported for transparency at the level of national government.

a) Investment by established foreign-controlled enterprises

None.

b) Corporate organisations

Air transport

Foreign-controlled enterprises, regardless of the degree of control, may register their aircraft in the national Register on the condition that national interests predominate in their administration and management. Such is the case when the majority of administrators, including the chairman and his deputy, as well as two-thirds of the members of the board of directors, are Italian nationals.

Authority: Article 143 of the Navigation Code.

Maritime transport

Foreign-controlled companies, regardless of the level of control, may have their ships entered in the national register on the condition that there is a predominance of national interests in their administration and direction. This is defined as arising when the majority of administrators, including the chairman and his deputy, as well as the majority of the board of directors, are Italian nationals.

Authority: Article 143 of the Navigation Code.

c) *Government purchasing*

None.

d) *Official aids and subsidies*

None.

B. **Measures reported for transparency at the level of territorial subdivisions**

None.

Annex 2

Statistics on Italy's foreign direct investment

Table 1. **Statistical indicators on foreign direct investment**

In US$ million

	1975-1980 average	1981	1982	1983	1984	1985	1986	1987	1988	1989	1990	1991	1992
Inflows of FDI	559	1 153	605	1 200	1 329	1 071	−21	4 144	6 882	2 181	6 344	2 481	3 161
Inflow growth (%)	..	106.2	−47.5	98.3	10.8	−19.4	−102.0	19 833.3	66.1	−68.3	190.9	−60.9	27.4
Outflows of FDI	421	1 425	1 025	2 133	2 012	1 820	2 652	2 339	5 554	2 135	7 612	7 326	5 956
Outflow growth (%)	..	238.5	−28.1	108.1	−5.7	−9.5	45.5	−11.8	137.5	−61.6	256.5	−3.8	−18.7
Net flows	138	−272	−420	−933	−683	−749	−2 673	1 805	1 328	46	−1 268	−4 845	−2 795
GDP	298 286	408 204	403 046	417 050	413 077	424 512	603 633	759 066	838 829	869 813	1 095 122	1 149 902	1 222 962
GDP nominal growth (%)	21.3	19.7	17.5	16.2	14.6	11.7	11.0	9.3	11.0	9.3	9.9	8.7	5.7
GDP real growth (%)	3.5	0.6	0.2	1.0	2.7	2.6	2.9	3.1	4.1	2.9	2.1	1.3	0.9
GFCF	70 518	97 367	90 006	88 779	86 856	87 771	119 166	149 762	168 446	175 661	221 973	227 124	233 732
GFCF growth (%)	..	38.1	−7.6	−1.4	−2.2	1.1	35.8	25.7	12.5	4.3	26.4	2.3	2.9
Inflows of FDI as % of GDP	0.2	0.3	0.2	0.3	0.3	0.3	0.0	0.5	0.8	0.3	0.6	0.2	0.3
Outflows of FDI as % of GDP	0.1	0.3	0.3	0.5	0.5	0.4	0.4	0.3	0.7	0.2	0.7	0.6	0.5
Inflows of FDI as % of GFCF	0.8	1.2	0.7	1.4	1.5	1.2	0.0	2.8	4.1	1.2	2.9	1.1	1.4
Outflows of FDI as % of GFCF	0.6	1.5	1.1	2.4	2.3	2.1	2.2	1.6	3.3	1.2	3.4	3.2	2.5

Sources: Banca d'Italia; OECD National Accounts; OECD Economic Outlook.

Table 2. Foreign direct investment flows by industry, 1980-1992

In L billion

	1980-1985 average	% of total	1986-1992 average	% of total	1986	1987	1988	1989	1990	1991	1992
Primary	113	7.8	275	6.0	218	385	607	81	251	-107	492
Agriculture	1	0.1	3	0.1	-	2	10	9	1	-3	3
Mining and quarrying	:	:	:	:	:	:	:	:	:	:	:
Oil[1]	111	7.7	272	5.9	218	383	597	72	250	-104	489
Secondary	775	53.7	1 610	35.0	-1 914	2 196	4 044	1 920	476	2 688	1 859
Food, beverages and tobacco	97	6.7	295	6.4	19	167	541	-138	773	135	567
Textiles, leather and clothing	15	1.1	111	2.4	36	117	-87	782	-134	74	-8
Paper, printing and publishing	:	:	:	:	:	:	:	:	:	:	:
Chemical products	239	16.6	586	12.7	466	379	1 052	946	48	1 150	64
Coal and petroleum products	:	:	:	:	:	:	:	:	:	:	:
Non-metallic products	:	:	:	:	:	:	:	:	:	:	:
Metal products	88	6.1	194	4.2	226	116	174	442	162	76	160
Mechanical equipment[2]	280	19.4	29	0.6	-2 831	706	1 884	-579	894	30	97
Electric and electronic equipment	:	:	:	:	:	:	:	:	:	:	:
Motor vehicles	:	:	:	:	:	:	:	:	:	:	:
Other transport equipment	:	:	:	:	:	:	:	:	:	:	:
Other manufacturing	56	3.9	395	8.6	170	711	480	467	-1 267	1 223	979
Tertiary	555	38.4	2 716	59.0	1 673	2 683	4 251	1 459	6 842	571	1 535
Construction	25	1.7	:	:	:	:	:	:	:	:	:
Wholesale and retail trade	113	7.8	416	9.0	184	368	1 469	177	578	90	44
Transport and storage	6	0.4	:	:	:	:	:	:	:	:	:
Finance, insurance and business services	306	21.2	2 106	45.8	1 307	1 623	2 570	323	7 123	148	1 651
Communication[3]	36	2.5	105	2.3	22	45	188	573	-132	30	8
Other services	69	4.8	89	1.9	160	647	24	386	-727	303	-168
Unallocated	1	0.1	1	0.03				9			
Total	1 443	100.0	4 603	100.0	-23	5 264	8 902	3 469	7 569	3 152	3 886

1. Including fuel and power products.
2. Including means of transport.
3. Including transport services.
Source: Banca d'Italia, Annual Report, various issues.

Table 3. **Outflows of Italian direct investment by industry, 1980-1992**

In L billion

	1980-1985 average	% of total	1986-1992 average	% of total	1986	1987	1988	1989	1990	1991	1992
Primary	639	27.7	163	2.8	212	143	41	304	248	47	144
Agriculture	1	0.0	24	0.4	10	1	1	170	50	-82	16
Mining and quarrying	:	:	:	:	:	:	:	:	:	:	:
Oil[1]	638	27.7	139	2.4	202	142	40	134	198	129	128
Secondary	521	22.6	1 072	18.4	1 096	1 108	548	294	1 397	2 137	921
Food, beverages and tobacco	9	0.4	158	2.7	23	73	-308	23	256	70	970
Textiles, leather and clothing	1	0.1	66	1.1	14	24	5	18	47	305	50
Paper, printing and publishing	:	:	:	:	:	:	:	:	:	:	:
Chemical products	101	4.4	205	3.5	310	851	373	-291	252	65	-127
Coal and petroleum products	:	:	:	:	:	:	:	:	:	:	:
Non-metallic products	:	:	:	:	:	:	:	:	:	:	:
Metal products	21	0.9	122	2.1	5	48	3	380	48	50	319
Mechanical equipment	102	4.4	286	4.9	333	-193	-123	514	420	1 040	14
Electric and electronic equipment	:	:	:	:	:	:	:	:	:	:	:
Motor vehicles	:	:	:	:	:	:	:	:	:	:	:
Other transport equipment	205	8.9	91	1.6	148	27	265	86	111	:	:
Other manufacturing	82	3.6	143	2.5	263	278	333	-436	263	607	-305
Tertiary	1 146	49.7	4 581	78.7	2 660	1 766	6 505	2 131	7 037	6 093	5 876
Construction	-3	-0.1	35	0.6	:	:	1 784	216	295	246	-141
Wholesale and retail trade	103	4.5	583	10.0	874	866	:	:	:	184	:
Transport and storage	5	0.2	:	:	:	:	:	:	:	:	:
Finance, insurance and business services	872	37.8	3 156	54.2	1 411	489	2 600	1 512	5 411	5 168	5 499
Communication[2]	11	0.5	173	3.0	25	6	1	203	189	126	660
Other services	158	6.9	635	10.9	350	405	2 120	200	1 142	369	-142
Unallocated	:	:	3	0.05	:	:	:	19	:	:	:
Total	2 306	100.0	5 818	100.0	3 968	3 017	7 094	2 748	8 682	8 277	6 941

1. Including fuel and power products.
2. Including transport services.
Source: Banca d'Italia, Annual Report, various issues.

56

Table 4. **Stocks of foreign direct investment: position at year-end by industry, 1980-1992**

In L billion

	1980-1985 average	% of total	1986-1992 average	% of total	1986	1987	1988	1989	1990	1991	1992
Primary	738	5.8	1 938	3.5	1 247	1 298	1 866	2 031	2 269	2 162	2 693
Agriculture	24	0.2	62	0.1	35	45	58	61	80	77	78
Mining and quarrying	..	..	..	..	..	..	..	..	..	..	..
Oil[1]	714	5.6	1 876	3.4	1 212	1 253	1 808	1 970	2 189	2 085	2 615
Secondary	7 221	56.6	25 169	45.3	20 997	18 354	25 256	28 952	25 055	27 772	29 797
Food, beverages and tobacco	457	3.6	2 443	4.4	901	1 218	2 059	2 700	3 028	3 163	4 033
Textiles, leather and clothing	315	2.5	1 131	2.0	1 105	660	904	1 456	1 215	1 289	1 285
Paper, printing and publishing	..	..	..	..	..	..	..	..	..	..	..
Chemical products	2 032	15.9	6 867	12.4	5 477	4 249	7 323	8 602	7 310	7 640	7 467
Coal and petroleum products	..	..	..	..	..	..	..	..	..	..	..
Non-metallic products	..	..	..	..	..	..	..	..	..	..	..
Metal products	150	1.2	530	1.0	321	324	399	608	597	673	789
Mechanical equipment	2 438	19.1	7 342	13.2	6 724	7 038	7 160	6 911	7 295	8 094	8 175
Electric and electronic equipment	..	..	..	..	..	..	..	..	..	..	..
Motor vehicles	..	..	..	..	..	..	..	..	..	..	..
Other transport equipment	1 101	8.6	3 142	5.7	4 354	2 808	3 688	4 282	2 110	2 341	2 413
Other manufacturing	728	5.7	3 714	6.7	2 115	2 057	3 723	4 393	3 500	4 572	5 635
Tertiary	4 791	37.6	28 474	51.2	12 461	17 008	21 040	31 768	38 208	38 750	40 080
Construction	916	7.2	3 660	6.6	2 054	2 693	3 201	3 655	4 596	4 686	4 738
Wholesale and retail trade	..	..	..	..	..	..	..	..	..	..	..
Transport and storage	..	..	..	..	..	..	..	..	..	..	..
Finance, insurance and business services	2 501	19.6	19 158	34.5	7 073	11 179	12 489	21 452	26 783	26 931	28 199
Communication[2]	189	1.5	944	1.7	645	261	415	1 399	1 218	1 248	1 419
Other services	1 185	9.3	4 712	8.5	2 689	2 875	4 935	5 262	5 611	5 885	5 724
Unallocated	..	..	..	..	..	..	..	..	..	..	..
Total	12 750	100.0	55 581	100.0	34 705	36 660	48 162	62 751	65 532	68 684	72 570

1. Including fuel and power products.
2. Including transport services.
Source: Banca d'Italia, Annual Report, various issues.

Table 5. Stocks of Italian direct investment abroad: position at year-end by industry, 1980-1992

In L billion

	1980-1985 average	% of total	1986-1992 average	% of total	1986	1987	1988	1989	1990	1991	1992
Primary	2 535	19.6	4 886	8.8	4 616	4 358	4 780	4 614	5 181	5 253	5 397
Agriculture	3	0.02	114	0.2	54	54	104	98	212	130	146
Mining and quarrying											
Oil[1]	2 533	19.6	4 772	8.6	4 562	4 304	4 676	4 516	4 969	5 123	5 251
Secondary	4 617	35.8	18 214	32.8	10 141	12 593	15 636	19 385	21 309	23 911	24 525
Food, beverages and tobacco	263	2.0	1 571	2.8	1 431	1 387	1 372	1 442	1 419	1 489	2 458
Textiles, leather and clothing	146	1.1	704	1.3	453	391	610	668	716	1 021	1 071
Paper, printing and publishing											
Chemical products	1 197	9.3	4 694	8.4	2 073	4 250	5 157	5 175	5 587	5 652	4 963
Coal and petroleum products											
Non-metallic products											
Metal products	590	4.6	1 374	2.5	611	1 236	1 470	1 484	1 460	1 510	1 849
Mechanical equipment	831	6.4	3 453	6.2	2 445	2 045	2 522	3 482	3 991	4 868	4 816
Electric and electronic equipment											
Motor vehicles											
Other transport equipment	987	7.6	1 706	3.1	1 545	1 412	1 715	1 559	1 640	2 001	2 067
Other manufacturing	604	4.7	4 712	8.5	1 583	1 872	2 790	5 575	6 496	7 370	7 301
Tertiary	5 760	44.6	32 483	58.4	20 144	20 334	27 776	30 352	36 917	43 012	48 847
Construction											
Wholesale and retail trade	563	4.4	4 042	7.3	2 507	2 885	4 992	4 269	4 549	4 734	4 361
Transport and storage											
Finance, insurance and business services	4 982	38.6	25 884	46.6	16 551	16 774	21 678	24 249	28 324	34 055	39 555
Communication[2]	73	0.6	493	0.9	132	148	349	335	526	649	1 309
Other services	142	1.1	2 064	3.7	954	527	757	1 499	3 518	3 574	3 622
Unallocated											
Total	12 912	100.0	55 583	100.0	34 901	37 285	48 192	54 351	63 407	72 176	78 769

1. Including fuel and power products.
2. Including transport services.
Source: Banca d'Italia, Annual Report, various issues.

58

Table 6. Inflows of foreign direct investment by country, 1982-1992

In L billion

	1982-1986 average	% of total	1987-1992 average	% of total	1987	1988	1989	1990	1991	1992
OECD AREA	1 567	114.8	5 064	94.2	4 880	9 201	3 495	7 358	2 233	3 217
Europe	997	73.0	4 157	77.3	3 780	7 521	2 303	7 001	2 013	2 325
EEC[1]	878	64.3	2 711	50.4	2 694	4 165	2 583	2 970	1 618	2 235
Belgium-Luxembourg	-18	-1.3	-58	-1.1	233	579	-2 933	239	960	577
Denmark	2	0.1	38	0.7	8	13	13	18	175	2
France	189	13.8	1 393	25.9	923	1 301	1 680	2 534	841	1 081
Germany	81	6.0	360	6.7	346	470	842	349	5	148
Greece	:	:	-7	-0.1	:	:	-1	4	-42	-
Ireland	6	0.5	:	-	:	19	1	65	-74	-11
Netherlands	239	17.5	419	7.8	725	945	997	-562	157	251
Portugal	-0.2	-0.01	6	0.1	21	17	:	10	12	13
Spain	5	0.4	42	0.8	21	17	65	-1	106	45
United Kingdom	374	27.4	517	9.6	438	821	1 919	314	-522	129
Other Europe	119	8.7	1 446	26.9	1 086	3 356	-280	4 031	395	90
North America	575	42.1	739	13.7	1 029	1 571	849	92	65	827
Canada	13	1.0	70	1.3	14	321	19	40	-	27
United States	562	41.2	669	12.4	1 015	1 250	830	52	65	800
Other OECD countries	-5	-0.4	168	3.1	71	109	343	265	155	65
Australia[2]	-9	-0.6	23	0.4	12	1	3	-16	139	-2
Japan	4	0.3	151	2.8	58	107	340	280	54	67
Turkey	0.2	0.01	-6	-0.1	1	1	:	1	-38	-
NON-OECD AREA	-202	-14.8	311	5.8	384	-299	-26	211	919	679
Central and Eastern Europe	:	:	124	2.3	2	2	1	29	3	708
Middle East	-294	-21.5	16	0.3	99	69	15	9	-83	-16
Other countries	92	6.8	172	3.2	283	-370	-42	173	999	-13
Total	1 365	100.0	5 375	100.0	5 264	8 902	3 469	7 569	3 152	3 896

1. In 1984 and 1988, EEC also includes European Institutions.
2. New Zealand included in Australian figure.
Source: Eurostat Questionnaire A: Direct Investment Capital and Income Flows.

Table 7. **Outflows of Italian direct investment by country, 1982-1992**

In L billion

	1982-1986 average	% of total	1987-1992 average	% of total	1987	1988	1989	1990	1991	1992
OECD AREA	2 254	72.4	4 168	67.7	2 246	4 715	2 247	7 970	1 561	6 270
Europe	1 639	52.7	3 744	60.8	2 046	4 261	3 641	7 244	1 275	3 996
EEC[1]	1 505	48.4	3 622	58.9	1 917	4 209	3 086	6 975	1 113	4 434
Belgium-Luxembourg	414	13.3	770	12.5	237	879	811	3 900	-1 264	58
Denmark	2	0.1	5	0.08	2	1	14	-6	3	17
France	218	7.0	782	12.7	564	839	590	920	89	1 688
Germany	146	4.7	267	4.3	182	119	313	812	226	-48
Greece	8	0.3	23	0.4	3	12	25	20	69	11
Ireland	1	0.04	10	0.2	12	8	2	14	-1	22
Netherlands	383	12.3	870	14.1	329	1 053	739	548	820	1 733
Portugal	6	0.2	70	1.1	4	6	8	18	24	361
Spain	77	2.5	297	4.8	558	121	137	302	182	480
United Kingdom	241	7.7	383	6.2	26	327	447	433	951	112
Other Europe	134	4.3	122	2.0	129	52	555	269	162	-438
North America	599	19.2	276	4.5	171	460	-1 876	400	286	2 212
Canada	63	2.0	19	0.3	21	14	34	47	13	-16
United States	535	17.2	257	4.2	150	446	-1 910	353	273	2 228
Other OECD countries	16	0.5	149	2.4	29	-6	482	326	-	62
Australia[2]	-8	-0.3	17	0.3	8	19	10	60	5	-2
Japan	24	0.8	105	1.7	13	-3	355	243	-25	45
Turkey	0.4	0.01	28	0.4	8	-22	117	23	20	19
NON-OECD AREA	859	27.6	1 986	32.3	771	2 379	501	480	6 716	1 070
Central and Eastern Europe	6	0.2	53	0.9	16	13	68	56	44	120
Middle East	186	6.0	3	0.05	153	120	16	-46	-200	-25
Other countries	667	21.4	1 930	31.4	602	2 246	417	470	6 872	975
Total	3 112	100.0	6 154	100.0	3 017	7 094	2 748	8 450	8 277	7 340

1. In 1984 and 1988, EEC also includes European Institutions.
2. New Zealand included in Australian figure.
Source: Eurostat Questionnaire A: Direct Investment Capital and Income Flows.

Table 8. Stocks of foreign direct investment: position at year-end by country, 1982-1992

In L billion

	1982-1986 average	% of total	1987-1992 average	% of total	1987	1988	1989	1990	1991	1992
OECD AREA	12 357	55.6	56 728	96.1	34 248	46 105	60 498	63 600	66 406	69 510
Europe	10 044	45.2	47 162	79.9	28 329	38 355	50 048	52 938	55 554	57 748
EEC[1]	10 979	49.4	30 819	52.2	19 839	25 967	33 266	32 870	35 434	37 540
Belgium-Luxembourg	1 482	6.7	5 094	8.6	4 026	5 282	5 466	4 306	5 452	6 029
Denmark	7	0.03	43	0.1	21	34	45	65	44	46
France	1 184	5.3	7 439	12.6	3 947	5 298	6 657	8 684	9 509	10 536
Germany	1 373	6.2	4 995	8.5	4 242	4 347	5 517	5 237	5 240	5 386
Greece	19	0.1	37	0.1	48	49	49	53	12	12
Ireland	7	0.03	35	0.1	17	33	33	98	11	18
Netherlands	1 647	7.4	6 736	11.4	4 157	5 683	7 873	7 221	7 669	7 813
Portugal	..	..	10	0.02	1	1	2	1	13	40
Spain	92	0.4	131	0.2	30	65	116	105	211	257
United Kingdom	1 214	5.5	6 304	10.7	3 350	5 175	7 508	7 115	7 273	7 403
Other Europe	3 018	13.6	16 343	27.7	8 490	12 388	16 782	20 068	20 120	20 208
Switzerland	2 378	10.7	13 029	22.1	6 196	9 700	13 551	16 195	16 282	16 247
North America	2 223	10.0	8 740	14.8	5 661	7 303	9 667	9 614	9 676	10 521
Canada	67	0.3	258	0.4	194	260	279	261	261	292
United States	2 156	9.7	8 483	14.4	5 467	7 043	9 388	9 353	9 415	10 229
Other OECD countries	90	0.4	826	1.4	258	447	783	1 048	1 176	1 241
Australia[2]	4	0.02	57	0.1	12	42	48	33	103	102
Japan	85	0.4	764	1.3	244	401	731	1 011	1 064	1 130
Turkey	1	0.003	5	0.01	2	4	4	4	9	9
NON-OECD AREA	954	4.3	2 332	3.9	2 412	2 057	2 253	1 932	2 278	3 060
Africa	30	0.1	251	0.4	63	144	177	121	510	488
Central and Eastern Europe	8	0.04	76	0.1	34	35	38	242	52	53
Latin America-Caribbean	401	1.8	871	1.5	958	1 124	1 175	820	721	430
Middle East	430	1.9	364	0.6	355	504	517	344	232	234
South and South East Asia	33	0.1	251	0.4	124	85	124	223	550	398
Other countries	53	0.2	520	0.9	878	165	222	182	213	1 457
Total	22 240	100.0	59 060	100.0	36 660	48 162	62 751	65 532	68 684	72 570

1. In 1984 and 1988, EEC also includes European Institutions.
2. New Zealand included in Australian figure.
Source: Banca d'Italia, Annual Report, various issues.

Table 9.   **Stocks of Italian direct investment abroad: position at year-end by country, 1982-1992**

In L billion

	1982-1986 average	% of total	1987-1992 average	% of total	1987	1988	1989	1990	1991	1992
OECD AREA	8 873	39.5	48 136	81.5	28 944	37 828	44 096	52 672	58 667	66 611
Europe	6 976	31.0	40 300	68.3	23 674	30 256	36 591	44 108	49 473	57 696
EEC[1]	8 966	39.9	32 689	55.4	17 524	23 753	29 127	35 917	40 617	49 195
Belgium-Luxembourg	2 035	9.1	9 937	16.8	5 593	7 363	8 071	11 342	12 368	14 882
Denmark	7	0.03	37	0.06	22	23	35	41	44	59
France	838	3.7	5 080	8.6	2 678	3 734	5 035	5 375	5 786	7 869
Germany	562	2.5	3 873	6.6	2 134	2 733	3 780	4 598	4 915	5 080
Greece	16	0.1	112	0.2	41	79	78	98	165	212
Ireland	22	0.1	93	0.2	77	79	98	113	64	126
Netherlands	1 187	5.3	6 416	10.9	3 430	4 656	5 854	6 380	7 925	10 253
Portugal	10	0.04	153	0.3	47	53	44	62	93	618
Spain	299	1.3	3 171	5.4	1 599	2 242	2 579	3 831	4 161	4 611
United Kingdom	586	2.6	3 758	6.4	1 903	2 791	3 553	3 717	5 096	5 485
Other Europe	1 414	6.3	7 611	12.9	6 150	6 503	7 464	8 191	8 856	8 501
Switzerland	1 322	5.9	7 032	11.9	5 890	6 147	6 843	7 296	8 131	7 885
North America	1 670	7.4	6 378	10.8	4 631	6 515	5 811	6 711	7 412	7 190
Canada	141	0.6	583	1.0	390	569	614	637	652	635
United States	1 529	6.8	5 796	9.8	4 241	5 946	5 197	6 074	6 760	6 555
Other OECD countries	227	1.0	1 458	2.5	639	1 057	1 694	1 853	1 782	1 725
Australia[2]	63	0.3	264	0.4	222	252	236	273	302	296
Japan	87	0.4	538	0.9	160	216	685	785	711	671
Turkey	76	0.3	655	1.1	257	589	772	789	769	753
NON-OECD AREA	3 580	15.9	10 894	18.5	8 341	10 364	10 255	10 735	13 509	12 157
Africa	251	1.1	1 216	2.1	844	866	559	1 085	1 952	1 989
Central and Eastern Europe	4	0.02	135	0.2	16	34	90	116	216	335
Latin America-Caribbean	2 333	10.4	6 277	10.6	5 682	6 937	6 521	6 582	5 868	6 074
Middle East	723	3.2	1 651	2.8	1 730	2 006	2 024	2 095	1 021	1 029
South and South East Asia	264	1.2	608	1.0	450	496	955	726	476	547
Other countries	6	0.03	1 007	1.7	-381	25	106	131	3 976	2 183
Total	22 475	100.0	59 030	100.0	37 285	48 192	54 351	63 407	72 176	78 768

1. In 1984 and 1988, EEC also includes European Institutions.
2. New Zealand included in Australian figure.
Source: Banca d'Italia, Annual Report, various issues.

Annex 3

Statistics on direct investment flows in OECD countries

Table 1. Foreign direct investment in OECD countries: inflows 1971-1992[1]

US$ million

	Cumulative flows		Flows of foreign direct investment											
	1971-1980	1981-1990	1981	1982	1983	1984	1985	1986	1987	1988	1989	1990	1991	1992
Australia	11 295	39 965	2 349	2 286	2 994	428	2 099	3 457	3 872	7 892	7 718	6 870	4 763	4 947
Austria	1 455	3 274	318	207	219	116	169	181	402	437	578	647	359	940
Belgium-Luxembourg[2]	9 215	28 182	1 352	1 390	1 271	360	957	631	2 338	4 990	6 731	8 162	8 919	10 791
Canada[2]	5 534	11 448	-3 670	-831	243	1 313	-2 050	990	3 469	3 614	1 773	6 597	6 544	4 963
Denmark	1 561	3 388	100	136	64	9	109	161	88	504	1 084	1 133	1 530	1 015
Finland	376	2 838	99	-4	84	138	110	340	265	530	489	787	-247	396
France[2]	16 908	43 194	2 426	1 563	1 631	2 198	2 210	2 749	4 621	7 204	9 552	9 040	11 073	15 894
Germany	13 969	18 029	341	819	1 775	553	587	1 190	1 901	1 203	7 131	2 529	4 263	2 422
Greece	..	6 145	520	436	439	485	447	471	683	907	752	1 005	1 135	1 144
Iceland[2]	..	12			..	14	23	8	2	-14	-27	6	35	17
Ireland	1 659	1 212	204	241	168	119	159	-43	89	91	85	99	97	102
Italy[2]	5 698	24 888	1 153	605	1 200	1 329	1 071	-21	4 144	6 882	2 181	6 344	2 481	3 161
Japan[2]	1 424	3 281	189	439	416	-10	642	226	1 165	-485	-1 054	1 753	1 368	2 728
Mexico	..	24 178	2 835	1 900	2 192	1 542	1 984	2 401	2 635	2 880	3 176	2 633	4 762	4 393
Netherlands	10 822	27 850	1 520	965	757	587	641	1 861	2 307	4 077	6 370	8 765	4 934	5 883
New Zealand	2 598	3 945	177	275	243	119	227	390	238	156	434	1 686	1 695	1 089
Norway	3 074	4 831	686	424	336	-210	-412	1 023	184	285	1 511	1 004	-291	720
Portugal[3]	535	6 256	177	145	150	170	218	166	367	692	1 577	2 594	3 168	2 994
Spain[2]	7 060	46 000	1 714	1 801	1 647	1 773	1 945	3 442	4 548	7 016	8 433	13 681	10 423	8 115
Sweden	897	8 676	182	361	223	290	396	1 079	646	1 661	1 809	2 029	6 315	241
Switzerland	..	12 432		..	286	520	1 050	1 778	2 044	42	2 254	4 458	2 613	465
Turkey[4]	228	2 340	95	55	46	113	99	125	106	354	663	684	810	844
United Kingdom	40 503	130 477	5 891	5 286	5 132	-241	5 780	8 557	15 450	21 356	30 369	32 897	15 934	18 165
United States	56 276	368 309	25 195	13 810	11 518	25 567	20 490	36 145	59 581	58 571	69 010	48 422	25 446	3 388
Total	188 249	821 150	43 853	32 309	33 034	37 282	38 951	67 307	111 145	130 845	162 599	163 825	118 129	94 817

1. Data updated in June 1994. Including data for Mexico who became a Member of OECD on 18 May 1994.
2. Reinvested earnings are not included in national statistics.
3. Figures for Portugal are only available from 1975 onward.
4. Cumulated inflows since 1954.

Source: OECD/DAF – Based on official national statistics from the balance of payments converted in US$ at daily average exchange rate.

Table 2. **Foreign direct investment in OECD countries: inflows 1981-1992**[1]

As a percentage of GDP

	1981	1982	1983	1984	1985	1986	1987	1988	1989	1990	1991	1992
Australia	1.4	1.4	1.8	0.2	1.3	2.1	2.0	3.2	2.7	2.3	1.6	1.7
Austria	0.5	0.3	0.3	0.2	0.3	0.2	0.3	0.3	0.5	0.4	0.2	0.5
Belgium-Luxembourg[2]	1.3	1.6	1.5	0.4	1.1	0.5	1.6	3.2	4.2	4.1	4.3	4.7
Canada[2]	-1.2	-0.3	0.1	0.4	-0.6	0.3	0.8	0.7	0.3	1.2	1.1	0.9
Denmark	0.2	0.2	0.1	0.0	0.2	0.2	0.1	0.5	1.0	0.9	1.2	0.7
Finland	0.2	0.0	0.2	0.3	0.2	0.5	0.3	0.5	0.4	0.6	-0.2	0.4
France[2]	0.4	0.3	0.3	0.4	0.4	0.4	0.5	0.7	1.0	0.8	0.9	1.2
Germany	0.1	0.1	0.3	0.1	0.1	0.1	0.2	0.1	0.6	0.2	0.3	0.1
Greece	1.4	1.1	1.3	1.4	1.3	1.2	1.5	1.7	1.4	1.5	1.6	1.5
Iceland[2]	0.0	0.0	0.0	0.5	0.8	0.2	0.0	-0.2	-0.5	0.1	0.5	0.3
Ireland	1.1	1.3	0.9	0.7	0.8	-0.2	0.3	0.3	0.2	0.2	0.2	0.2
Italy[2]	0.3	0.2	0.3	0.3	0.3	-0.0	0.5	0.8	0.3	0.6	0.2	0.3
Japan[2]	0.0	0.0	0.0	-0.0	0.0	0.0	0.0	-0.0	-0.0	0.1	0.0	0.1
Mexico	1.2	1.9	1.8	1.0	1.9	2.8	3.0	1.7	1.7	1.1	1.7	1.3
Netherlands	1.1	0.7	0.6	0.5	0.5	1.0	1.1	1.8	2.8	3.1	1.7	1.8
New Zealand	0.7	1.2	1.0	0.5	1.0	1.4	0.7	0.4	1.0	3.9	4.0	2.6
Norway	1.2	0.8	0.6	-0.4	-0.7	1.5	0.2	0.3	1.7	1.0	-0.3	0.6
Portugal	0.7	0.6	0.7	0.9	1.1	0.6	1.0	1.7	3.5	4.3	4.6	3.6
Spain[2]	0.9	1.0	1.0	1.1	1.2	1.5	1.6	2.0	2.2	2.8	2.0	1.4
Sweden	0.2	0.4	0.2	0.3	0.4	0.8	0.4	0.9	0.9	0.9	2.6	0.1
Switzerland	0.0	0.0	0.3	0.6	1.1	1.3	1.2	0.0	1.3	2.0	1.1	0.2
Turkey	0.2	0.1	0.1	0.2	0.2	0.2	0.2	0.5	0.8	0.6	0.7	0.8
United Kingdom	1.2	1.1	1.1	-0.1	1.3	1.5	2.2	2.6	3.6	3.4	1.6	1.7
United States	0.8	0.4	0.3	0.7	0.5	0.9	1.3	1.2	1.3	0.9	0.5	0.1

1. Data updated in June 1994. Including data for Mexico who became a Member of OECD on 18 May 1994.
2. Reinvested earnings are not included in national statistics.
Source: OECD/DAF – Based on official national statistics from the balance of payments.

Table 3. Direct investment abroad from OECD countries: outflows 1971-1992[1]

US$ million

	Cumulative flows		Flows of direct investment abroad											
	1971-1980	1981-1990	1981	1982	1983	1984	1985	1986	1987	1988	1989	1990	1991	1992
Australia	2 510	23 102	734	693	518	1 402	1 887	3 419	5 096	5 074	3 267	1 012	2 026	–197
Austria	578	4 132	206	142	190	68	74	313	312	309	855	1 663	1 288	1 871
Belgium-Luxembourg[2]	3 213	21 454	30	–77	358	282	231	1 627	2 680	3 609	6 114	6 600	6 062	10 891
Canada[2]	11 335	39 571	5 756	709	2 758	2 277	2 855	4 066	7 069	5 278	4 603	4 200	5 409	3 723
Denmark	1 063	6 292	141	77	159	93	303	646	618	719	2 027	1 509	1 851	2 225
Finland	605	12 132	129	85	143	493	352	810	1 141	2 608	3 108	3 263	1 049	406
France[2]	13 940	85 618	4 615	3 063	1 841	2 126	2 226	5 230	8 704	12 756	18 137	26 920	20 501	19 097
Germany	24 846	86 573	3 860	2 481	3 170	4 389	4 804	9 616	9 105	11 431	14 549	23 168	22 879	17 715
Iceland[2]	..	27					..	2	7	1	8	9	10	27
Italy[2]	3 597	28 707	1 425	1 025	2 133	2 012	1 820	2 652	2 339	5 554	2 135	7 612	7 326	5 956
Japan[2]	18 052	185 826	4 894	4 540	3 612	5 965	6 452	14 480	19 519	34 210	44 130	48 024	30 726	17 222
Netherlands	27 829	52 952	3 629	2 610	2 098	2 530	2 829	3 147	7 087	4 073	11 521	13 428	11 997	12 669
New Zealand	375	4 563	103	87	404	31	174	87	562	615	135	2 365	1 472	391
Norway	1 079	8 995	185	317	360	612	1 228	1 605	890	968	1 352	1 478	1 840	434
Portugal[3]	21	374	16	9	17	8	15	–2	–16	77	85	165	474	719
Spain[2]	1 274	8 196	272	505	245	249	252	377	754	1 227	1 470	2 845	3 574	1 273
Sweden	4 597	47 725	854	1 237	1 459	1 506	1 783	3 947	4 789	7 468	10 189	14 493	7 026	1 219
Switzerland	..	31 858	..	..	492	1 139	4 572	1 461	1 274	8 696	7 852	6 372	6 543	4 899
Turkey[4]	..	–7							9	–	–	–16	27	65
United Kingdom	55 112	185 674	12 065	7 145	8 211	8 039	10 818	17 077	31 308	37 110	35 172	18 729	15 597	16 571
United States	134 354	171 626	9 623	1 078	6 686	11 649	12 724	17 706	28 980	17 871	37 604	27 705	32 098	37 122
Total	**302 306**	**1 005 390**	**48 537**	**25 726**	**34 854**	**44 870**	**55 399**	**88 266**	**132 227**	**159 654**	**204 313**	**211 544**	**179 775**	**154 298**

1. Data updated in June 1994. No data available on outflows for Mexico.
2. Reinvested earnings are not included in national statistics.
3. Figures for Portugal are only available from 1975 onward.
4. Includes cumulative investment since 1954.
Source: OECD/DAF – Based on official national statistics from the balance of payments converted in US$ at daily average exchange rate.

Table 4. Direct investment abroad from OECD countries: outflows 1981-1992[1]

As a percentage of GDP

	1981	1982	1983	1984	1985	1986	1987	1988	1989	1990	1991	1992
Australia	0.4	0.4	0.3	0.8	1.2	2.0	2.6	2.0	1.2	0.3	0.7	-0.1
Austria	0.3	0.2	0.3	0.1	0.1	0.3	0.3	0.2	0.7	1.0	0.8	1.0
Belgium-Luxembourg[2]	0.0	-0.1	0.4	0.4	0.3	1.4	1.8	2.3	3.8	3.3	2.9	4.7
Canada[2]	2.0	0.2	0.8	0.7	0.8	1.1	1.7	1.1	0.8	0.7	0.9	0.7
Denmark	0.2	0.1	0.3	0.2	0.5	0.8	0.6	0.7	1.9	1.2	1.4	1.6
Finland	0.3	0.2	0.3	1.0	0.7	1.2	1.3	2.5	2.7	2.4	0.9	0.4
France[2]	0.8	0.6	0.4	0.4	0.4	0.7	1.0	1.3	1.9	2.3	1.7	1.4
Germany	0.6	0.4	0.5	0.7	0.8	1.1	0.8	1.0	1.2	1.5	1.4	1.0
Iceland[2]	0.0	0.0	0.0	0.0	0.0	0.1	0.1	0.0	0.1	0.1	0.2	0.4
Italy[2]	0.3	0.3	0.5	0.5	0.4	0.4	0.3	0.7	0.2	0.7	0.6	0.5
Japan[2]	0.4	0.4	0.3	0.5	0.5	0.7	0.8	1.2	1.5	1.6	0.9	0.5
Netherlands	2.5	1.9	1.5	2.0	2.2	1.8	3.3	1.8	5.0	4.7	4.1	4.0
New Zealand	0.4	0.4	1.7	0.1	0.8	0.3	1.5	1.4	0.3	5.4	3.5	0.9
Norway	0.3	0.6	0.7	1.1	2.1	2.3	1.1	1.1	1.5	1.4	1.7	0.4
Portugal	0.1	0.0	0.1	0.0	0.1	0.0	-0.0	0.2	0.2	0.3	0.7	0.9
Spain[2]	0.1	0.3	0.2	0.2	0.2	0.2	0.3	0.4	0.4	0.6	0.7	0.2
Sweden	0.7	1.2	1.6	1.6	1.8	3.0	3.0	4.1	5.3	6.3	2.9	0.5
Switzerland	0.0	0.0	0.5	1.3	4.9	1.1	0.7	4.7	4.4	2.8	2.8	2.0
Turkey	0.0	0.0	0.0	0.0	0.0	0.0	0.0	0.0	0.0	0.0	0.0	0.1
United Kingdom	2.4	1.5	1.8	1.9	2.4	3.0	4.5	4.4	4.2	1.9	1.5	1.6
United States	0.3	0.0	0.2	0.3	0.3	0.4	0.6	0.4	0.7	0.5	0.6	0.6

1. Data updated in June 1994. No data available on outflows for Mexico.
2. Reinvested earnings are not included in national statistics.

Source: OECD/DAF – Based on official national statistics from the balance of payments.

MAIN SALES OUTLETS OF OECD PUBLICATIONS
PRINCIPAUX POINTS DE VENTE DES PUBLICATIONS DE L'OCDE

ARGENTINA – ARGENTINE
Carlos Hirsch S.R.L.
Galería Güemes, Florida 165, 4° Piso
1333 Buenos Aires   Tel. (1) 331.1787 y 331.2391
Telefax: (1) 331.1787

AUSTRALIA – AUSTRALIE
D.A. Information Services
648 Whitehorse Road, P.O.B 163
Mitcham, Victoria 3132   Tel. (03) 873.4411
Telefax: (03) 873.5679

AUSTRIA – AUTRICHE
Gerold & Co.
Graben 31
Wien I   Tel. (0222) 533.50.14

BELGIUM – BELGIQUE
Jean De Lannoy
Avenue du Roi 202
B-1060 Bruxelles   Tel. (02) 538.51.69/538.08.41
Telefax: (02) 538.08.41

CANADA
Renouf Publishing Company Ltd.
1294 Algoma Road
Ottawa, ON K1B 3W8   Tel. (613) 741.4333
Telefax: (613) 741.5439
Stores:
61 Sparks Street
Ottawa, ON K1P 5R1   Tel. (613) 238.8985
211 Yonge Street
Toronto, ON M5B 1M4   Tel. (416) 363.3171
Telefax: (416)363.59.63

Les Éditions La Liberté Inc.
3020 Chemin Sainte-Foy
Sainte-Foy, PQ G1X 3V6   Tel. (418) 658.3763
Telefax: (418) 658.3763

Federal Publications Inc.
165 University Avenue, Suite 701
Toronto, ON M5H 3B8   Tel. (416) 860.1611
Telefax: (416) 860.1608

Les Publications Fédérales
1185 Université
Montréal, QC H3B 3A7   Tel. (514) 954.1633
Telefax : (514) 954.1635

CHINA – CHINE
China National Publications Import
Export Corporation (CNPIEC)
16 Gongti E. Road, Chaoyang District
P.O. Box 88 or 50
Beijing 100704 PR   Tel. (01) 506.6688
Telefax: (01) 506.3101

DENMARK – DANEMARK
Munksgaard Book and Subscription Service
35, Nørre Søgade, P.O. Box 2148
DK-1016 København K   Tel. (33) 12.85.70
Telefax: (33) 12.93.87

FINLAND – FINLANDE
Akateeminen Kirjakauppa
Keskuskatu 1, P.O. Box 128
00100 Helsinki

Subscription Services/Agence d'abonnements :
P.O. Box 23
00371 Helsinki   Tel. (358 0) 12141
Telefax: (358 0) 121.4450

FRANCE
OECD/OCDE
Mail Orders/Commandes par correspondance:
2, rue André-Pascal
75775 Paris Cedex 16   Tel. (33-1) 45.24.82.00
Telefax: (33-1) 49.10.42.76
Telex: 640048 OCDE

OECD Bookshop/Librairie de l'OCDE :
33, rue Octave-Feuillet
75016 Paris   Tel. (33-1) 45.24.81.67
(33-1) 45.24.81.81
Documentation Française
29, quai Voltaire
75007 Paris   Tel. 40.15.70.00
Gibert Jeune (Droit-Économie)
6, place Saint-Michel
75006 Paris   Tel. 43.25.91.19
Librairie du Commerce International
10, avenue d'Iéna
75016 Paris   Tel. 40.73.34.60
Librairie Dunod
Université Paris-Dauphine
Place du Maréchal de Lattre de Tassigny
75016 Paris   Tel. (1) 44.05.40.13
Librairie Lavoisier
11, rue Lavoisier
75008 Paris   Tel. 42.65.39.95
Librairie L.G.D.J. - Montchrestien
20, rue Soufflot
75005 Paris   Tel. 46.33.89.85
Librairie des Sciences Politiques
30, rue Saint-Guillaume
75007 Paris   Tel. 45.48.36.02
P.U.F.
49, boulevard Saint-Michel
75005 Paris   Tel. 43.25.83.40
Librairie de l'Université
12a, rue Nazareth
13100 Aix-en-Provence   Tel. (16) 42.26.18.08
Documentation Française
165, rue Garibaldi
69003 Lyon   Tel. (16) 78.63.32.23
Librairie Decitre
29, place Bellecour
69002 Lyon   Tel. (16) 72.40.54.54

GERMANY – ALLEMAGNE
OECD Publications and Information Centre
August-Bebel-Allee 6
D-53175 Bonn   Tel. (0228) 959.120
Telefax: (0228) 959.12.17

GREECE – GRÈCE
Librairie Kauffmann
Mavrokordatou 9
106 78 Athens   Tel. (01) 32.55.321
Telefax: (01) 36.33.967

HONG-KONG
Swindon Book Co. Ltd.
13–15 Lock Road
Kowloon, Hong Kong   Tel. 366.80.31
Telefax: 739.49.75

HUNGARY – HONGRIE
Euro Info Service
Margitsziget, Európa Ház
1138 Budapest   Tel. (1) 111.62.16
Telefax : (1) 111.60.61

ICELAND – ISLANDE
Mál Mog Menning
Laugavegi 18, Pósthólf 392
121 Reykjavik   Tel. 162.35.23

INDIA – INDE
Oxford Book and Stationery Co.
Scindia House
New Delhi 110001   Tel.(11) 331.5896/5308
Telefax: (11) 332.5993
17 Park Street
Calcutta 700016   Tel. 240832

INDONESIA – INDONÉSIE
Pdii-Lipi
P.O. Box 269/JKSMG/88
Jakarta 12790   Tel. 583467
Telex: 62 875

ISRAEL
Praedicta
5 Shatner Street
P.O. Box 34030
Jerusalem 91430   Tel. (2) 52.84.90/1/2
Telefax: (2) 52.84.93
R.O.Y.
P.O. Box 13056
Tel Aviv 61130   Tél. (3) 49.61.08
Telefax (3) 544.60.39

ITALY – ITALIE
Libreria Commissionaria Sansoni
Via Duca di Calabria 1/1
50125 Firenze   Tel. (055) 64.54.15
Telefax: (055) 64.12.57
Via Bartolini 29
20155 Milano   Tel. (02) 36.50.83
Editrice e Libreria Herder
Piazza Montecitorio 120
00186 Roma   Tel. 679.46.28
Telefax: 678.47.51
Libreria Hoepli
Via Hoepli 5
20121 Milano   Tel. (02) 86.54.46
Telefax: (02) 805.28.86
Libreria Scientifica
Dott. Lucio de Biasio 'Aeiou'
Via Coronelli, 6
20146 Milano   Tel. (02) 48.95.45.52
Telefax: (02) 48.95.45.48

JAPAN – JAPON
OECD Publications and Information Centre
Landic Akasaka Building
2-3-4 Akasaka, Minato-ku
Tokyo 107   Tel. (81.3) 3586.2016
Telefax: (81.3) 3584.7929

KOREA – CORÉE
Kyobo Book Centre Co. Ltd.
P.O. Box 1658, Kwang Hwa Moon
Seoul   Tel. 730.78.91
Telefax: 735.00.30

MALAYSIA – MALAISIE
Co-operative Bookshop Ltd.
University of Malaya
P.O. Box 1127, Jalan Pantai Baru
59700 Kuala Lumpur
Malaysia   Tel. 756.5000/756.5425
Telefax: 757.3661

MEXICO – MEXIQUE
Revistas y Periodicos Internacionales S.A. de C.V.
Florencia 57 - 1004
Mexico, D.F. 06600   Tel. 207.81.00
Telefax : 208.39.79

NETHERLANDS – PAYS-BAS
SDU Uitgeverij Plantijnstraat
Externe Fondsen
Postbus 20014
2500 EA's-Gravenhage   Tel. (070) 37.89.880
Voor bestellingen: Telefax: (070) 34.75.778

NEW ZEALAND
NOUVELLE-ZÉLANDE
Legislation Services
P.O. Box 12418
Thorndon, Wellington   Tel. (04) 496.5652
Telefax: (04) 496.5698

NORWAY – NORVÈGE
Narvesen Info Center – NIC
Bertrand Narvesens vei 2
P.O. Box 6125 Etterstad
0602 Oslo 6   Tel. (022) 57.33.00
     Telefax: (022) 68.19.01

PAKISTAN
Mirza Book Agency
65 Shahrah Quaid-E-Azam
Lahore 54000   Tel. (42) 353.601
     Telefax: (42) 231.730

PHILIPPINE – PHILIPPINES
International Book Center
5th Floor, Filipinas Life Bldg.
Ayala Avenue
Metro Manila   Tel. 81.96.76
     Telex 23312 RHP PH

PORTUGAL
Livraria Portugal
Rua do Carmo 70-74
Apart. 2681
1200 Lisboa   Tel.: (01) 347.49.82/5
     Telefax: (01) 347.02.64

SINGAPORE – SINGAPOUR
Gower Asia Pacific Pte Ltd.
Golden Wheel Building
41, Kallang Pudding Road, No. 04-03
Singapore 1334   Tel. 741.5166
     Telefax: 742.9356

SPAIN – ESPAGNE
Mundi-Prensa Libros S.A.
Castelló 37, Apartado 1223
Madrid 28001   Tel. (91) 431.33.99
     Telefax: (91) 575.39.98

Libreria Internacional AEDOS
Consejo de Ciento 391
08009 – Barcelona   Tel. (93) 488.30.09
     Telefax: (93) 487.76.59
Llibreria de la Generalitat
Palau Moja
Rambla dels Estudis, 118
08002 – Barcelona
     (Subscripcions) Tel. (93) 318.80.12
     (Publicacions) Tel. (93) 302.67.23
     Telefax: (93) 412.18.54

SRI LANKA
Centre for Policy Research
c/o Colombo Agencies Ltd.
No. 300-304, Galle Road
Colombo 3   Tel. (1) 574240, 573551-2
     Telefax: (1) 575394, 510711

SWEDEN – SUÈDE
Fritzes Information Center
Box 16356
Regeringsgatan 12
106 47 Stockholm   Tel. (08) 690.90.90
     Telefax: (08) 20.50.21

Subscription Agency/Agence d'abonnements :
Wennergren-Williams Info AB
P.O. Box 1305
171 25 Solna   Tel. (08) 705.97.50
     Téléfax : (08) 27.00.71

SWITZERLAND – SUISSE
Maditec S.A. (Books and Periodicals - Livres
et périodiques)
Chemin des Palettes 4
Case postale 266
1020 Renens   Tel. (021) 635.08.65
     Telefax: (021) 635.07.80

Librairie Payot S.A.
4, place Pépinet
CP 3212
1002 Lausanne   Tel. (021) 341.33.48
     Telefax: (021) 341.33.45

Librairie Unilivres
6, rue de Candolle
1205 Genève   Tel. (022) 320.26.23
     Telefax: (022) 329.73.18

Subscription Agency/Agence d'abonnements :
Dynapresse Marketing S.A.
38 avenue Vibert
1227 Carouge   Tel.: (022) 308.07.89
     Telefax : (022) 308.07.99

See also – Voir aussi :
OECD Publications and Information Centre
August-Bebel-Allee 6
D-53175 Bonn (Germany)   Tel. (0228) 959.120
     Telefax: (0228) 959.12.17

TAIWAN – FORMOSE
Good Faith Worldwide Int'l. Co. Ltd.
9th Floor, No. 118, Sec. 2
Chung Hsiao E. Road
Taipei   Tel. (02) 391.7396/391.7397
     Telefax: (02) 394.9176

THAILAND – THAÏLANDE
Suksit Siam Co. Ltd.
113, 115 Fuang Nakhon Rd.
Opp. Wat Rajbopith
Bangkok 10200   Tel. (662) 225.9531/2
     Telefax: (662) 222.5188

TURKEY – TURQUIE
Kültür Yayinlari Is-Türk Ltd. Sti.
Atatürk Bulvari No. 191/Kat 13
Kavaklidere/Ankara   Tel. 428.11.40 Ext. 2458
Dolmabahce Cad. No. 29
Besiktas/Istanbul   Tel. 260.71.88
     Telex: 43482B

UNITED KINGDOM – ROYAUME-UNI
HMSO
Gen. enquiries   Tel. (071) 873 0011
Postal orders only:
P.O. Box 276, London SW8 5DT
Personal Callers HMSO Bookshop
49 High Holborn, London WC1V 6HB
     Telefax: (071) 873 8200
Branches at: Belfast, Birmingham, Bristol, Edin-
burgh, Manchester

UNITED STATES – ÉTATS-UNIS
OECD Publications and Information Centre
2001 L Street N.W., Suite 700
Washington, D.C. 20036-4910 Tel. (202) 785.6323
     Telefax: (202) 785.0350

VENEZUELA
Libreria del Este
Avda F. Miranda 52, Aptdo. 60337
Edificio Galipán
Caracas 106   Tel. 951.1705/951.2307/951.1297
     Telegram: Libreste Caracas

Subscription to OECD periodicals may also be
placed through main subscription agencies.

Les abonnements aux publications périodiques de
l'OCDE peuvent être souscrits auprès des
principales agences d'abonnement.

Orders and inquiries from countries where Distribu-
tors have not yet been appointed should be sent to:
OECD Publications Service, 2 rue André-Pascal,
75775 Paris Cedex 16, France.

Les commandes provenant de pays où l'OCDE n'a
pas encore désigné de distributeur devraient être
adressées à : OCDE, Service des Publications,
2, rue André-Pascal, 75775 Paris Cedex 16, France.

9-1994

OECD PUBLICATIONS, 2 rue André-Pascal, 75775 PARIS CEDEX 16
PRINTED IN FRANCE
(21 94 52 1) ISBN 92-64-14217-7 - No. 47449 1994
ISSN 1021-5794